101 Fun Things to do in Retirement

Spice Up Your Golden Years, Escape the Ordinary andEmbrace the Extraordinary!

Jeffrey C. Chapman

Contents

Please Consider Leaving a Review

Hello there!

As an author, I know just how important reviews are for getting the word out about my work. When readers leave a review on Amazon or any other book stores, it helps others discover my book and decide whether it's right for them.

Plus, it gives me valuable feedback on what readers enjoyed and what they didn't.

So if you've read my book and enjoyed it, I would really appreciate it if you took a moment to leave a review on Amazon. It doesn't have to be long or complicated - just a few words about what you thought of the book would be incredibly helpful.

Thank you so much for your support!

Jeff

Introduction

Remember how time warped as a kid? Summers stretched into blissful eternities, while the school year felt like a decade trapped in slow motion. Then suddenly, with a blink and a poof of pension plan paperwork, you're retired. The good news: It's the ultimate break from routine! The slightly daunting news: Turns out, freedom on tap needs some focus to be truly fulfilling.

You've put in the work, earned every minute of this next chapter, and yet, no guidebook magically appears alongside your first senior discount card. Well, consider this your guidebook! Think of it as your roadmap for turning those wide-open days into adventures big and small. Inside, you'll find 101 ways to add a dash of unexpected to the ordinary, rekindle passions that got put on hold, and discover new talents that might just surprise you.

Whether it's taking on a totally new challenge, finally exploring that place you've always dreamed of, or simply finding ways to connect and contribute in your community, this book is your nudge, your cheerleader, and your toolbox for making retirement the most vibrant, joyful, "HECK YES!" chapter of your life. So, go on, turn the page and let the fun begin!

Creative Arts

Wearable Art Workshops

Ditch the Snooze-Worthy Sweats: Embrace Your Inner Fashion Weirdo with Wearable Art Workshops

Brief Description:

FORGET BORING BASICS! TRANSFORM your wardrobe from "blah" to "ta-dah!" with wearable art workshops. Get messy, get creative, and express your quirky side as you turn plain clothes into walking (and wearable) masterpieces. Paint a silly slogan on a t-shirt, bedazzle your tote bag, or upcycle that hideous sweater into a surprisingly wearable work of art.

Why It's Great for Retirees:

- **Permission to be playful:** Retirement is the perfect time to let loose and try something a little ridiculous.

- **Combat "old person style":** Who needs sensible shoes when you can rock hand-painted sneakers?

- **Conversation starter:** Your mismatched, paint-splattered outfits are guaranteed to get people talking (and maybe even complimenting!).

- **Practical jokes galore:** Upcycle your friend's least favorite shirt into something even more outrageous and gift it back.

Getting Started:

- **Embrace the mess:** Wear clothes you don't mind ruining or invest in a giant, ridiculous apron.

- **Lower your expectations:** The goal is self-expression, not runway-ready fashion. The uglier, the better!

- **Gather your weapons of choice:** Fabric paints, glitter, old jewelry, feathers...the weirder, the better!

Resources Needed:

- **Local art spaces:** Check for workshops with titles like "Messy Mondays" or "Upcycle Your Ugly Clothes."

- **Youtube tutorials:** Search for "fashion disasters turned fabulous" for questionable inspiration.

- **Thrift stores:** A treasure trove of hideous items begging for your creative touch.

- **A sense of humor:** Leave your fashion inhibitions at the door.

Challenges and Tips:

- **The dreaded "craft fail":** If it's wearable and makes you laugh, it's a success!

- **Fabric paint mishaps:** Oops, spilled paint on the carpet? Call it abstract art.

- **Fear of looking ridiculous:** That's the whole point! Own your unique style.

Ways to Deepen the Experience:

- **Theme nights:** Host a wearable art party where everyone turns up in their most outlandish creations.

- **Fashion challenges:** Transform thrift store finds into wearable outfits with a time limit.

- **Start a "bad fashion" blog:** Document your hilarious creations and inspire others to unleash their inner fashion disasters.

Safety and Accessibility:

- **Ventilate your workspace:** Fabric paint fumes can make you a little loopy (in a fun way!).

- **Opt for fabric-safe glues:** Avoid hot glue gun mishaps near your favorite body parts.

- **Accessibility options:** Check for adapted tools and wheelchair-friendly spaces.

Call to Action:

Ready to unleash your inner fashion disaster (and secretly love it)? Find a wearable art workshop today and let the creative chaos begin!

Interactive Art Installations

Step Inside the Art: Interactive Installations That Will Blow Your Mind (and Get You Moving)

Brief Description:

FORGET STARING AT PAINTINGS – interactive art installations invite you to become part of the artwork! Imagine walls that light up with your touch, sculptures that respond to your voice, or digital projections that dance along with your movements. Get ready to play, explore, and unleash your inner child as you experience art in a whole new way.

Why It's Great for Retirees:

- **A Workout Without the Gym:** These installations encourage movement, play, and a sense of wonder – all disguised as fun!

- **Tech Without the Fear:** Discover the playful side of technology in a way that's intuitive and engaging.

- **Rediscover Your Inner Artist:** Even if you can't draw a stick figure, you can leave your mark on these ever-changing artworks.

- **Unleash the Grandkids' Envy:** The next time they visit, trade museum tours for an interactive art adventure that's cooler than any video game.

Getting Started:

- **Seek Out Installations:** Museums, galleries, and community spaces are increasingly hosting interactive exhibitions. Keep an eye on local events listings.

- **Do Your Research:** Check out artists' websites or videos of past installations to see what might appeal to you.

- **Dress for Adventure:** Comfy clothes and sneakers are your best bet for installations that encourage movement.

Resources Needed:

- **Local Museums/Galleries:** Check their websites for schedules and interactive exhibits.

- **Festival Listings:** Many cities host digital art festivals that feature cutting-edge installations.

- **Interactive Artist Websites:** Discover artists who specialize in this field and look for upcoming shows near you.

Challenges and Tips

- **Tech Hesitation:** Don't be afraid! Most installations are designed to be user-friendly with playful instructions.

- **Crowds:** Visit during weekdays or off-peak hours for a more relaxed experience.

- **Overstimulation:** Take breaks if needed – some installations can be intense!

Ways to Deepen the Experience:

- **Learn the Basics:** Take a workshop on coding, 3D modeling, or electronics to design your own simple installations.

- **Behind the Scenes Tours:** Some spaces offer talks with the artists for deeper insights into their process.

- **Host an "Art Playdate":** Invite friends for a shared interactive art experience followed by a lively discussion.

Safety and Accessibility:

- **Check for Restrictions:** Some installations may have restrictions on age, mobility, or light/sound sensitivity.

- **Respect the Space:** Follow guidelines for interacting with the artwork to ensure its longevity.

- **Be Aware of Surroundings:** Get carried away with the experience but stay alert to avoid bumping into others.

Call to Action:

Ready to step out of your comfort zone and into a whole new world of art? Find an interactive art installation near you and prepare to be amazed!

3

Art from Nature

Ditch the Paintbrushes, Channel Your Inner Forest Goblin: Art from Nature Retreats

Brief Description:

Escape the studio and let Mother Nature be your muse! In these Art from Nature retreats, you'll transform leaves, twigs, stones, and other natural treasures into whimsical creations. Embrace the beauty of imperfection and tap into a sense of childlike wonder as you connect with your inner artist and the world around you.

Why It's Great for Retirees:

- **Mindful Meditation in Motion:** Slow down, observe the details of nature, and lose yourself in the creative flow.

- **Zero Art Skills Required:** It's about the playful process, not polished masterpieces.

- **Leave No Trace Adventures:** Connect with nature without harming it, sparking environmental awareness with a creative twist.

- **Storytelling Treasures:** Each piece you create comes with a unique tale from your nature adventure.

Getting Started:

- **Embrace Impermanence:** Nature art is often fleeting – take photos or simply enjoy the moment of creation.

- **Choose Your Adventure:** Beaches, forests, and meadows each offer unique materials and inspire different moods.

- **Pack Light, Think Playful:** A tote bag for your finds and a sense of curiosity are all you need.

Resources Needed:

- **Nature Retreat Centers:** Look for locations with easy access to varied natural environments.

- **Workshop Leaders:** Seek out naturalists who also have artistic or creative backgrounds.

- **Online Inspiration:** Search "nature art" or "land art" for ideas to spark your imagination.

Challenges and Tips:

- **Weather woes:** Embrace the elements – bring layers and be ready to channel your inner rain-splashed mud creature.

- **Inspiration Drought:** Start small. Sometimes a single beautiful rock or seashell is your launchpad.

- **"Is this even art?":** Silence your inner critic and celebrate the joy of the process.

Ways to Deepen the Experience:

- **Nature Journaling:** Combine sketching and writing with your art-making for deeper reflection.

- **Group Collaborations:** Build a giant nature mandala or a "fairy village" together.

- **Pop-Up Gallery:** Display your creations (temporarily!) along a trail for others to discover.

Safety and Accessibility:

- **Know Your Limits:** Choose terrain that suits your fitness level.

- **Plant and Critter Smarts:** Workshops should include basic identification to avoid poisonous plants or disturbing wildlife.

- **Leave It As You Found It:** Mindful harvesting and careful placement ensure you leave the site pristine.

Call to Action:

Ready to channel your inner forest goblin and let nature surprise you? Find an Art from Nature retreat and unleash your wild creative spirit!

4

Virtual Reality Art Galleries

Escape the Ordinary: Step into Virtual Reality Art Galleries Where Imagination Reigns Supreme

Brief Description:

FORGET STUFFY MUSEUMS AND limited gallery space. Virtual Reality (VR) Art Galleries shatter the boundaries of the traditional art world. Immerse yourself in boundless digital landscapes where sculptures float mid-air, paintings morph and change, and the very laws of physics are playfully bent. Experience a global art scene from the comfort of your home.

Why It's Great for Retirees:

- **Travel without Leaving Home:** Explore cutting-edge art from around the world without the hassle of flights and crowds.

- **A Feast for the Senses:** VR galleries can incorporate sound, movement, and even interactive elements, engaging you on a deeper level.

- **Democratizing Art:** VR makes art accessible to those with limited mobility or who live far from major cultural hubs.

- **Supporting Emerging Artists:** Discover exciting new talent from around the world on the virtual stage.

Getting Started:

- **The Gear:** Start with a basic VR headset (many are smartphone-compatible) or upgrade for a more immersive experience.

- **Explore VR Gallery Apps:** Platforms like VR-All-Art: https://vrallart.com/ offer a curated selection of virtual exhibitions.

- **Artist Websites:** Many contemporary artists now build VR components into their online portfolios.

Resources Needed:

- **VR Headset Comparison Guides:** Websites like CNET or Tom's Guide can help you choose the right headset for your budget and needs.

- **VR Art Communities:** Join online forums or social media groups to discover new exhibitions and artists.

- **Tech Support:** Enlist a tech-savvy friend or relative to get you set up if it feels intimidating.

Challenges and Tips:

- **Motion Sickness:** Start with short VR sessions and choose experiences with gentle movement.

- **Loneliness Factor:** Host virtual gallery tours with friends for a shared social experience.

- **Finding the Good Stuff:** It's still the wild west of VR art, so be prepared for mixed quality alongside hidden gems.

Ways to Deepen the Experience:

- **Behind the Scenes with Artists:** Seek out galleries that offer VR artist talks or studio tours.

- **Create Your Own VR Art:** Explore simple 3D modeling tools to turn your doodles into virtual sculptures.

- **Host a VR Art Party:** Invite friends for a shared virtual gallery experience followed by a lively discussion.

Safety and Accessibility:

- **Clear Your Space:** Make sure you have room to move around safely while wearing your headset.

- **Seated Experiences:** Look for options that allow seated viewing for those with limited mobility.

- **Take Breaks:** Step away from the screen regularly to avoid eye strain and disorientation.

Call to Action:

Ready to step into a world where art transcends reality? Slip on your VR headset and begin your virtual art adventure!

5

Soundscapes

Become a Maestro of Mood: Discover the Magic of Soundscapes

Brief Description:

THE WORLD IS YOUR orchestra! With soundscape creation, you'll learn to capture the rustle of leaves, the buzz of a city street, or even the creak of your own floorboards, and transform them into auditory adventures. Compose soundscapes that transport listeners to another place, set a scene in their imagination, or stir deep emotions.

Why It's Great for Retirees:

- **Train Your Ears, Awaken Your Senses:** Rediscover the often-overlooked symphony of everyday sounds.

- **Technology as a Creative Tool:** Easy-to-use recording and editing apps put a soundscape studio in your pocket.

- **Storytelling Without Words:** Express yourself through a unique and evocative art form.

- **Meditation Reimagined:** Craft calming soundscapes to create your own sonic sanctuary.

Getting Started:

- **Embrace Your Inner Sound Hunter:** Take "listening walks" – parks, cafes, even your own home – and pay attention!

- **Simple Recording Tools:** Start with your smartphone's recording app or explore free options like Audacity.

- **Play!:** Experiment with layering sounds, adjusting speed, and adding simple effects.

Resources Needed:

- **Field Recording Guides:** Learn tips for capturing high-quality environmental sounds.

- **Free Audio Editing Software:** Explore beginner-friendly options for manipulating your sounds.

- **Soundscape Inspiration:** Listen to the work of sound artists or explore libraries of found sounds.

Challenges and Tips:

- **Background Noise:** Find quiet spots or learn simple editing techniques to reduce unwanted sounds.

- **The Blank Page Syndrome:** Start with a mood or theme (e.g., "bustling market", "calm rain") to spark ideas.

- **Overcomplicating It:** Simple is often better – a few well-chosen sounds can be incredibly powerful.

Ways to Deepen the Experience:

- **Collaborate:** Create a soundscape story with friends, each person adding a layer.

- **Score Your Memories:** Enhance old photos or home videos with a custom-made soundscape.

- **Mindfulness Practice:** Design soundscapes to accompany guided meditation or relaxation.

Safety and Accessibility:

- **Respectful Recording:** When recording in public, be mindful of others' privacy.

- **Headphone Awareness:** Use headphones at reasonable volumes to protect your ears.

- **Descriptive Show Notes:** Help visually impaired listeners by providing context for your soundscapes.

Call to Action:

Ready to turn the world into your sonic playground? Grab your recording device, tune your ears, and start creating auditory magic!

Street Art Tours and Workshops

Unleash Your Inner Urban Artist: Street Art Tours and Workshops

Brief Description:

Dive into the vibrant world of street art! Guided tours unveil the hidden stories and techniques behind those eye-catching murals and tags. Then, get your hands messy with workshops where you'll learn the basics of graffiti, stenciling, sticker art, and other expressive urban art forms.

Why It's Great for Retirees:

- **Discover a Hidden World:** Explore your city like never before, appreciating the often-overlooked art right in front of you.

- **Learn from the Experts:** Gain insights into the history, techniques, and social messages of street art.

- **Express Yourself in a New Way:** Whether you're a seasoned artist or a complete newbie, there's joy in creative experimentation.

- **Community Connection:** Meet like-minded art enthusiasts and perhaps contribute to the urban art scene yourself.

Getting Started:

- **Find Your Tours:** Search for "Street Art Tours" in your city, often offered by local artists or community groups.

- **Workshop Options:** Check if tour companies offer workshops, or seek out independent artist-led classes.

- **Basic Supplies:** Most workshops provide materials, but a sketchbook for ideas never hurts!

Resources Needed:

- **City-Specific Guides:** Search for street art maps or blogs highlighting local hotspots.

- **Street Art Documentaries:** Get inspired by films like "Exit Through the Gift Shop" or "Saving Banksy".

- **Artist Websites:** Follow the work of street artists who inspire you.

Challenges and Tips:

- **Respect the Streets:** Understand the unspoken rules of street art culture (e.g., don't paint over another artist's work without permission).

- **Start Small:** In workshops, practice on scrap materials before going big.

- **Embrace the Ephemeral:** The beauty of street art is its often temporary nature – let go of perfectionism.

Ways to Deepen the Experience:

- **Create Your Own Stickers:** Design eye-catching stickers and spread your art around town (responsibly!).

- **Advocate for Murals:** Support local initiatives that create legal spaces for street artists.

- **Mini Street Art Tour Host:** Lead your own tour for friends, sharing your newfound knowledge.

Safety and Accessibility:

- **Tour Awareness:** Stay alert in urban areas and follow the guide's instructions.

- **Workshop Chemicals:** Ask about proper ventilation and potential allergens in spray paints or glues.

- **Know the Laws:** Be aware of local restrictions on where you can practice street art.

Call to Action:

Ready to see your city in a whole new light and get your creative juices flowing? Find a street art tour and let the urban landscape become your canvas!

Recycled Metal Sculpture

Scrap Metal Masterpieces: Unleash Your Inner Welder with Recycled Sculpture Workshops

Brief Description:

Breathe new life into discarded metal! In these exhilarating workshops, you'll transform nuts, bolts, old tools, and other scrap metal into unique and expressive sculptures. Master the basics of welding and metalworking while embracing the unpredictable beauty that emerges from repurposed materials.

Why It's Great for Retirees:

- **The Thrill of Transformation:** Witness the magic of turning "junk" into art.

- **Learn Empowering Skills:** Welding opens a world of creative possibilities beyond sculpture.

- **Sustainable Art:** Celebrate eco-friendly expression while saving treasures from the landfill.

- **Embrace Imperfection:** The rough, industrial charm is part of the recycled metal aesthetic.

Getting Started:

- **Safety First:** Workshops should prioritize proper gear (helmet, gloves, etc.) and instruction.

- **Source Your Materials:** Junkyards, scrap heaps, and even your own garage are treasure troves.

- **Inspiration Station:** Before you weld, gather images of recycled metal sculptures to spark your imagination.

Resources Needed:

- **Workshop Spaces:** Look for community workshops, maker spaces, or artists offering classes.

- **Welding Equipment and Supplies:** Workshops should provide everything, but check for prerequisites.

- **Online Tutorials:** Supplement your learning with videos on basic welding techniques.

Challenges and Tips:

- **Heavy Lifting:** Ensure assistance is available if needed for moving larger pieces.

- **It Gets Hot:** Dress in layers you can shed and stay hydrated.

- **Start with Small Projects:** Build your confidence and skills before tackling grand sculptures.

Ways to Deepen the Experience:

- **Scavenger Hunts:** Turn sourcing materials into a fun group outing at flea markets and scrap yards.

- **Collaborative Creations:** Work with others to build large-scale, community sculptures.

- **Sell Your Sculptures:** Explore craft markets or online platforms to turn your hobby into a side hustle.

Safety and Accessibility:

- **Proper Ventilation:** Welding fumes require well-ventilated spaces.

- **Protective Gear:** Safety glasses, gloves, and welding masks are essential.

- **Modifications:** Instructors should adapt techniques or tools for those with limited strength or mobility

Call to Action:

Ready to spark some creative magic and transform scrap metal into stunning sculptures? Find a recycled metal workshop and unleash your inner metalworking maverick!

Experimental Film Making

Break the Mold: Discover the Wild World of Experimental Filmmaking

Brief Description:

FORGET TRADITIONAL STORYTELLING! IN this course, you'll dive into the exhilarating world of experimental filmmaking, where rules are meant to be shattered. Play with unconventional shooting techniques, explore nonlinear narratives, and manipulate images and sound to create films that are thought-provoking, visually arresting, and uniquely your own.

Why It's Great for Retirees:

- **Creative Liberation:** Embrace a sense of artistic freedom and challenge traditional filmmaking notions.

- **No Tech Expertise Needed:** Often, the simplest tools create the most striking experimental effects.

- **Express Yourself Uniquely:** Discover new ways to share your ideas, emotions, and experiences through film.

- **Join a Vibrant Community:** Connect with fellow filmmakers who push the boundaries of the medium.

Getting Started:

- **Think Like an Explorer:** Experiment with basic film effects like slow motion, reverse playback, and layering images.

- **Embrace Limitations:** Your smartphone can be a powerful tool for experimental filmmaking.

- **Seek Inspiration:** Watch experimental short films on platforms like Vimeo or at local film festivals.

Resources Needed:

- **Workshop Listings:** Check community art centers, film schools, or online platforms for courses.

- **Simple Editing Software:** Explore free or affordable options with intuitive interfaces.

- **Experimental Film Library:** Seek out online resources or books celebrating the history of the genre.

Challenges and Tips:

- **Let Go of Perfection:** Beauty lies in the unexpected. Embrace glitches and unplanned imperfections.

- **The Audience is YOU:** Focus on expressing yourself, not worrying about mainstream appeal.

- **Start Short and Sweet:** Create short, experimental pieces to build confidence and hone your skills.

Ways to Deepen the Experience:

- **Reimagine Old Footage:** Breathe new life into home videos or found footage with experimental editing.

- **Collaborate with Other Artists:** Combine your film with a poet's words or a musician's soundscape.

- **Host Screening Parties:** Share your creations with a community of open-minded viewers.

Safety and Accessibility:

- **Seizure Warnings:** Use flashing lights or fast-paced visuals responsibly with clear warnings.

- **Flexible Learning:** Courses with a mix of online and in-person components can provide broader access.

- **Supportive Community:** Seek out instructors who foster a safe space for experimentation and feedback.

Call to Action:

Ready to unleash your inner cinematic rebel? Find an experimental filmmaking course and begin crafting films that defy the ordinary!

9

Art Therapy Sessions

The Art of Healing: Discover the Transformative Power of Art Therapy Sessions

Brief Description:

ART THERAPY PROVIDES A safe space to express yourself without words. Guided by a trained therapist, you'll use painting, drawing, sculpting, and other creative processes to explore emotions, gain self-awareness, and nurture your emotional well-being. No artistic skill is required – the focus is on the journey, not the final product.

Why It's Great for Retirees:

- **Process Deep Emotions:** Retirement can trigger complex feelings – art therapy offers a healthy outlet for exploration.

- **Cope with Loss and Change:** Visual expression can aid in navigating grief, transitions, and challenging life events.

- **Reduced Stress and Anxiety:** The act of creating can be soothing and promote a sense of calm.

- **Self-Discovery and Empowerment:** Uncover hidden strengths and gain new perspectives on your life.

Getting Started:

- **Finding a Qualified Therapist:** Seek an art therapist with credentials in counseling or psychology (e.g., ATR-BC).

- **Openness to the Process:** Be willing to explore different art materials and trust the guidance of the therapist.

- **No Judgement Zone:** Art therapy is about self-expression, not creating masterpieces.

Resources Needed:

- **Art Therapy Organizations:** Look for national or regional associations and their therapist directories.

- **Local Support:** Check hospitals, community mental health centers, or art studios that offer art therapy.

- **Introductory Readings:** Books on art therapy can provide an overview before your first session.

Challenges and Tips:

- **Facing Difficult Emotions:** Art therapy can bring up strong feelings – know that the therapist is there to support you.

- **Trusting the Mess:** Embrace the imperfections and focus on the process of creating.

- **It's Not About "Art Skills":** Even stick figures can be a powerful tool for self-expression.

Ways to Deepen the Experience:

- **Keep a Visual Journal:** Continue simple art-making between sessions to track your inner world.

- **Mindful Art Observation:** Visit museums and focus on your emotional response to the artwork.

- **Combine with Traditional Talk Therapy:** Art therapy can be a powerful addition to a broader mental health plan.

Safety and Accessibility:

- **Trigger Warnings:** Therapists should be sensitive to potentially triggering themes or materials.

- **Physical Limitations:** Art therapy can be adapted to accommodate various physical abilities.

- **Respect for Privacy:** Sessions are confidential, creating a safe space for self-exploration.

Call to Action:

Ready to embark on a journey of healing and self-discovery through the power of art? Connect with a qualified art therapist and begin exploring your inner world through creative expression.

10

Culinary Art Experiences

Masterpieces on Your Plate: Culinary Art Experiences That Delight the Eye and the Palate

Brief Description:

ELEVATE YOUR COOKING BEYOND mere sustenance! In these culinary art experiences, you'll learn not just how to cook delicious food, but how to turn your dishes into edible masterpieces. Explore color, texture, plating techniques, and even edible garnishes for stunning presentations that transform meals into a feast for all the senses.

Why It's Great for Retirees:

- **Reignite Your Passion for Cooking:** Break out of recipe ruts and turn everyday meals into exciting events.

- **Mindful Eating with a Twist:** Develop mindfulness about the visual beauty and composition of your food.

- **Impress and Entertain:** Master plating techniques that will wow guests at your next dinner party.

- **Creative Expression on the Plate:** Tap into your artistic side in a delicious and edible medium.

Getting Started:

- **Inspiration is Everywhere:** Look at food magazines, cooking shows, and artistic plating photos online.

- **Simple Starts Big Impact:** Practice striking plate arrangements with even basic meals you already cook.

- **Play With Your Food:** Experiment with contrasting colors, textures, and edible garnishes like herbs or flowers.

Resources Needed:

- **Culinary Art Workshops:** Seek classes focused on presentation, not just traditional cooking techniques.

- **Food Styling Books:** Look for guides that provide inspiration and step-by-step visual instructions.

- **Plating Tools:** A few simple items like tweezers, squeeze bottles, or garnishing tools can elevate the experience.

Challenges and Tips:

- **Overcomplicating It:** Start with one statement element per plate and build from there.

- **Flavor Over Form:** Remember, it has to taste as good as it looks! Don't sacrifice flavor for the aesthetic.

- **Playful Imperfection:** Relax and enjoy the process. Edible art can have an organic beauty.

Ways to Deepen the Experience:

- **Themed Dinner Parties:** Design a whole menu around a color scheme, cultural cuisine, or artistic style.

- **Photography Fun:** Master food photography to capture your creations and share them with others.

- **Edible Landscapes:** Experiment with miniature food "sculptures" for a playful, whimsical presentation.

Safety and Accessibility:

- **Ingredient Awareness:** Be mindful of common allergies or sensitivities when sharing your creations.

- **Fresh and Vibrant:** Prioritize fresh ingredients for the most visually stunning results.

- **Adaptive Tools:** Seek out larger, easier-to-grip plating tools if dexterity is a concern.

Call to Action:

Ready to turn your kitchen into an artist's studio? Unleash your inner food stylist and start creating dishes that are as beautiful to behold as they are to eat!

Health and Fitness

11

Silent Disco Yoga

Find Your Flow in the Silent Disco: Experience the Joy of Silent Disco Yoga

Brief Description:

GET READY TO DITCH the quiet yoga studio and groove your way through a yoga flow! In Silent Disco Yoga, you'll wear wireless headphones playing upbeat, energizing music while a yoga instructor guides you through the poses. Lose yourself in the music, connect with your body, and enjoy a playful workout without noise distractions.

Why It's Great for Retirees:

- **Fun and Social Atmosphere:** The energetic music and disco vibe create a sense of community and lightheartedness.

- **No Judgement Zone:** Focus on your own practice without feeling self-conscious in a traditional quiet class.

- **Mind-Body Connection:** The immersive music experience helps you tune into your breath and body movements.

- **Accessible for All Levels:** The music creates a motivating rhythm while instructors often offer modifications.

Getting Started:

- **Find Your Party...er, Class:** Search for "Silent Disco Yoga" classes in your area, often offered at yoga studios or unique event spaces.

- **Comfy and Cool:** Wear comfortable yoga clothes and be prepared to sweat a little.

- **Open Mind = More Fun:** Embrace the unique experience and let yourself get a little silly!

Resources Needed:

- **Silent Disco Class Listings:** Check local yoga studios, event websites, and search online.

- **The Right Playlist:** Instructors curate playlists for different vibes (uplifting, chill, etc.), but feel free to suggest songs!

- **Studio Gear:** Most classes provide the headphones and yoga mats, but double-check when booking.

Challenges and Tips:

- **Headphone Hassle:** It can take a moment to get used to wearing headphones while moving.

- **Staying Focused:** The upbeat music can be distracting, remember to tune back into your breath.

- **Slippery Situation:** Avoid excessive lotion or oils beforehand, as sweaty headphones can be a hazard.

Ways to Deepen the Experience:

- **Themed Classes:** Look for classes with specific music eras or styles (80's pop, meditative beats, etc.).

- **Glow in the Flow:** Some events incorporate glow sticks and blacklights for extra disco vibes.

- **Instructor Collab:** Partner with a local yoga teacher to host your own Silent Disco Yoga events.

Safety and Accessibility:

- **Volume Control:** Participants can usually adjust headphone volume for comfort and safety.

- **Pace Modifications:** Instructors should offer variations for those who want a gentler practice.

- **Health Considerations:** Those with sensitivity to loud noise or flashing lights should consult a doctor first.

Call to Action:

Ready to shake up your yoga routine and unleash your inner dancing yogi? Find a Silent Disco Yoga class and prepare to flow to the beat!

12

Wilderness Survival Fitness

Unleash Your Inner Survivor: Wilderness Survival Fitness Retreats

Brief Description:

GET READY TO CONQUER not just your workouts, but the wild! These outdoor fitness retreats blend intense training with practical survival skills. Build strength, stamina, and agility through hikes, obstacle courses, and challenges inspired by real-world survival scenarios. Leave feeling stronger, more resilient, and ready for any adventure.

Why It's Great for Retirees:

- **Break Out of Gym Routines:** Ditch the treadmill for thrilling, ever-changing natural environments.

- **Functional Fitness for Life:** Develop strength and skills that translate to everyday confidence and resilience.

- **Rediscover Your Inner Strength:** Challenge yourself mentally and physically, unearthing hidden potential.

- **Build Community with Fellow Adventurers:** Bond with people who share your love of pushing boundaries.

Getting Started:

- **Assess Your Fitness Level:** Choose a retreat that aligns with your current abilities and offers options.

- **Pack for Adventure:** Proper gear, including sturdy footwear and hydration, is essential.

- **Prepare to be Challenged:** These retreats are about pushing your limits, safely and with expert guidance.

Resources Needed:

- **Retreat Locations:** Search for wilderness training centers, adventure travel companies, or fitness facilities offering specialized programs.

- **Qualified Instructors:** Prioritize experience in both fitness instruction and wilderness skills.

- **Safety Protocols:** Reputable retreats will have a solid plan for emergencies and group management.

Challenges and Tips:

- **Facing the Elements:** Be prepared for heat, cold, rain, and unpredictable terrain.

- **Pushing Past Your Comfort Zone:** Embrace the challenge and know that instructors are there for support.

- **Sore Muscles are a Badge of Honor:** Expect some aches – proper recovery is key between sessions.

Ways to Deepen the Experience:

- **Learn Primitive Skills:** Incorporate fire-building, shelter construction, or foraging into your training.

- **Focus on Agility and Balance:** Train on uneven terrain and natural obstacles to improve real-world resilience.

- **Mindset Matters:** Some retreats include elements of mental resilience and survival psychology training.

Safety and Accessibility:

- **Know Your Limits:** Honest self-assessment helps you choose the right retreat and avoid injuries.

- **Medical Disclaimers:** Retreats may require disclosing health conditions and getting a doctor's okay.

- **Adaptations Available:** Inquire about modifications if you have specific limitations or concerns.

Call to Action:

Ready to leave the gym behind and embrace your inner survivor? Find a Wilderness Survival Fitness retreat and unleash your wild potential!

13

Aqua Zumba

Make Waves of Fun: Dive into the Exhilaration of Aqua Zumba

Brief Description:

GET READY TO DITCH the dance floor and take your Zumba moves to the pool! Aqua Zumba combines the upbeat Latin rhythms and easy-to-follow choreography of Zumba with the low-impact benefits of water exercise. It's a party in the pool that burns calories, improves flexibility, and feels amazing!

Why It's Great for Retirees:

- **Easy on the Joints:** The buoyancy of water reduces stress on joints, making it ideal for those with arthritis or injuries.

- **Full Body Blast:** Water resistance adds an extra challenge, working your muscles in new ways.

- **Beat the Heat, Stay Cool:** The perfect way to stay active and have fun even on hot summer days.

- **Inclusive and Social:** The water creates a welcoming, playful environment for all fitness levels.

Getting Started:

- **Find Your Splash Zone:** Check pools, community centers, and gyms offering Aqua Zumba classes.

- **Just Add Water (and Comfy Clothes):** No fancy gear needed – a swimsuit and a smile are all it takes!

- **Listen to Your Body:** Start at your own pace and increase intensity gradually.

Resources Needed:

- **Class Listings:** Search for "Aqua Zumba near me" online or ask your local aquatic center.

- **Pool-tastic Tunes:** Instructors curate playlists specifically for the water workout experience.

- **Instructor Certification:** Ensure your instructor has the proper aquatic fitness training.

Challenges and Tips:

- **Coordination in the Currents:** Moving in water takes practice, so be patient and embrace a few giggles.

- **Slippery Situation:** Check if the pool has a textured bottom for better grip.

- **Drink Up:** It's easy to forget to hydrate, so bring a water bottle poolside.

Ways to Deepen the Experience:

- **Themed Classes:** Look for classes based on specific music styles (salsa, disco, even 80s throwbacks!).

- **Pool Party Vibes:** Encourage a social atmosphere with post-class smoothies or chats.

- **Expand Your Aquatic Adventures:** Try other water exercises like aqua aerobics or water jogging.

Safety and Accessibility:

- **Instructor Awareness:** Let your instructor know about any health conditions or limitations beforehand.

- **Stay Shallow (if needed):** Many moves can be modified in shallower water.

- **Flotation Aids:** Noodles or belts can add support or increase the challenge.

Call to Action:

Ready to shake things up and make your workouts a splash? Find an Aqua Zumba class and let the water work its fitness magic!

14

Parkour for Beginners

Unleash Your Inner Ninja: Parkour for Beginners – Build Strength, Agility, and Confidence

Brief Description:

EVER LOOK AT THE world and see a giant playground? Parkour is the art of moving through your environment with power, fluidity, and creativity. In this beginner workshop, you'll learn the fundamentals of safe parkour techniques, building strength, coordination, and the confidence to overcome obstacles both on and off the course.

Why It's Great for Retirees:

- **Functional Fitness:** Develop strength and agility that translate into greater everyday confidence.

- **Challenge Your Brain AND Body:** Parkour promotes problem-solving, spatial awareness, and quick thinking.

- **Rediscover Playfulness:** Tap into a childlike sense of exploration and fun movement.

- **Supportive Community:** Parkour fosters a strong sense of camaraderie and mentorship.

Getting Started:

- **Find a Qualified Instructor:** Experience in parkour AND teaching safe techniques is essential.

- **Start Slow and Safe:** Focus on mastering the basics before attempting complex moves.

- **Environment Matters:** Begin training in a controlled setting (gym with pads, low obstacles outdoors).

Resources Needed:

- **Parkour Workshops:** Search online or in your community specifically for beginner-level classes.

- **Comfortable Clothing:** Wear clothes you can move freely in and supportive sneakers.

- **Online Tutorials (With Caution):** Supplement your workshop with videos, but prioritize your instructor's guidance.

Challenges and Tips:

- **Fear Factor:** It's normal to hesitate! Start with small, achievable challenges and focus on proper technique.

- **Progression, Not Perfection:** Celebrate every little win and remember that practice makes progress.

- **Listen to Your Body:** Rest is key for avoiding injuries and enjoying the journey.

Ways to Deepen the Experience:

- **Parkour Playground Exploration:** Take field trips to find new spots to practice your skills safely in the real world.

- **Philosophy of Movement:** Learn about the history and values behind parkour as a discipline.

- **Collaborative Training:** Join groups or train with friends to share tips and motivation.

Safety and Accessibility:

- **Age is Just a Number:** Training can be adapted for any fitness level.

- **Injury Prevention Focus:** Emphasize warm-ups, cool-downs, and spotting techniques.

- **Honesty About Limitations:** Communicating physical concerns with your instructor is crucial.

Call to Action:

Ready to see your world in a whole new way? Find a Parkour for Beginners workshop and embrace the challenge of playful movement!

15

Dance-Walk Groups

Move, Explore, & Groove: Join the Dance-Walk Revolution!

Brief Description:

GET READY TO DITCH boring walks and turn them into joyful journeys! Dance-Walk groups combine the benefits of walking with the fun of spontaneous dance moves set to upbeat music. Explore your city, discover scenic trails, and let the rhythm be your guide.

Why It's Great for Retirees:

- **Low-Impact, High Fun Factor:** Enjoy exercise that feels more like a party than a workout.

- **Social Connection:** Meet like-minded people who love to move and laugh together.

- **Mood Booster:** Music and movement are a powerful combo for lifting your spirits.

- **Explore Your Surroundings:** Discover hidden gems and see familiar places with fresh eyes.

Getting Started:

- **Find Your Jam (and Group):** Look for organized Dance-Walk groups in your area or start your own!

- **Comfortable Footwear:** Supportive shoes are key for happy feet while you dance-walk.

- **Pump Up the Playlist:** Choose a mix of upbeat songs you can easily put simple moves to.

Resources Needed:

- **Community Groups:** Check social media, community centers, or dance studios for existing groups.

- **Portable Speaker:** Share your dance-walk soundtrack with the group.

- **Route Planning Apps:** Map out scenic trails or interesting city routes that allow for some grooving.

Challenges and Tips:

- **Self-Consciousness:** Start in less crowded spaces if you're shy and gradually build your confidence.

- **Creative Choreography:** Keep it simple! A few repeated moves to the music are all you need.

- **Vary Your Pace:** Alternate between brisk walking and spontaneous dance breaks for a good workout.

Ways to Deepen the Experience:

- **Themed Walks:** Choose eras (disco!), cultural dance styles, or movie soundtracks to inspire your moves.

- **Spontaneous Flash Mobs:** Add a touch of playful performance to your walk with a quick choreographed routine.

- **Sharing the Joy:** Dance-walk through senior centers to spread the fun and invite others to join.

Safety and Accessibility:

- **Choose Safe Routes:** Well-maintained paths and sidewalks are best for carefree movement.

- **Adjust the Intensity:** Encourage participants to listen to their bodies and modify as needed.

- **Hydration Breaks:** Make sure to schedule breaks for water and rest, especially in warm weather.

Call to Action:

Ready to add some rhythm to your step and laughter to your day? Find or start a Dance-Walk group and explore the world with a joyful bounce!

16

Mindful Movement Classes

Discover Inner Harmony: Mindful Movement Classes

Brief Description:

LET GO OF STRESS and cultivate a deep sense of calm with Mindful Movement classes. These classes combine gentle, flowing movements from practices like tai chi or qigong with guided mindfulness meditation. Learn to move with awareness, connect with your breath, and find a quiet space within.

Why It's Great for Retirees:

- **Improved Balance and Flexibility:** Slow, controlled movements enhance physical resilience.

- **Stress and Anxiety Relief:** Mindful focus on the breath calms the nervous system.

- **Enhanced Body Awareness:** Learn to tune in to subtle sensations and release tension.

- **Accessible for All:** Classes can be adapted to any fitness level or mobility restriction.

Getting Started:

- **Finding the Right Class:** Search for "Mindful Movement," "Tai Chi for Mindfulness," or "Qigong for Seniors" in your area.

- **Experienced Instructor:** Look for teachers with certifications and a focus on both movement and mindfulness principles.

- **Openness to Explore:** Be willing to try slow, meditative movement, even if it feels unfamiliar at first.

Resources Needed:

- **Studio or Community Class Listings:** Check local listings, yoga studios, or senior centers.

- **Online Classes:** Consider online platforms for guided practices you can do at home.

- **Comfortable Clothing:** Wear loose-fitting clothes that allow for easy movement.

Challenges and Tips:

- **Patience and Self-Compassion:** Don't focus on mastering the forms, emphasize the mindful experience itself.

- **Distracting Thoughts:** It's normal! Gently redirect your attention back to your breath and movement.

- **Find Your Pace:** Start with shorter sessions and gradually increase practice time.

Ways to Deepen the Experience:

- **Mindful Walking in Nature:** Take the principles outdoors by focusing on your senses while walking slowly.

- **Daily Mini-Practices:** Incorporate simple movements and breath awareness into your daily routine.

- **Explore the Philosophy:** Read about the origins and underlying principles of tai chi or qigong.

Safety and Accessibility:

- **Respect Your Limits:** Never push through pain - mindful movement should be gentle and comfortable.

- **Modifications Provided:** Instructors should offer adaptations for various fitness levels and abilities.

- **Health Considerations:** Check with your doctor if you have any health concerns before starting.

Call to Action:

Ready to find tranquility through movement and breath? Seek out a Mindful Movement class and embark on a journey of inner peace and well-being.

17

Virtual Reality Fitness Adventures

Escape the Gym, Conquer Virtual Worlds: VR Fitness Adventures

Brief Description:

GET READY TO DITCH your boring treadmill for fantastical journeys! With VR Fitness Adventures, you'll pedal, run, or row through stunning virtual landscapes, from mountain ranges to underwater realms. Turn your workout into an immersive adventure, making exercise anything but routine.

Why It's Great for Retirees:

- **Beat Workout Boredom:** Explore new worlds with each session, keeping workouts exciting and motivating.

- **Track Your Progress:** Many VR fitness experiences incorporate game-like elements and progress tracking.

- **Low-Impact Options:** Cycling and rowing in VR can be great alternatives for those with joint concerns.

- **Explore Without Leaving Home:** Travel the world virtually when real-world travel is difficult.

Getting Started:

- **The Gear:** Choose a VR headset compatible with fitness apps and your chosen workout (bike, treadmill, etc.).

- **Explore VR Fitness Apps:** Research options like VZFit, Holofit, and others offering diverse environments.

- **Set Up Your Space:** Ensure you have enough room for safe movement and equipment.

Resources Needed:

- **VR Headset Comparison Guides:** Websites like Tom's Guide can help you choose based on fitness needs.

- **VR Fitness App Reviews:** Search for specific workouts (cycling, etc.) and the experiences they offer.

- **Equipment Retailers:** If needed, purchase a stationary bike, specialized treadmill, or rowing machine.

Challenges and Tips:

- **Potential Motion Sickness:** Start with short sessions and choose less intense visuals.

- **Cost Factor:** VR headsets and associated equipment can be an investment.

- **Don't Neglect Your Form:** Focus on maintaining proper exercise form even with the immersive visuals.

Ways to Deepen the Experience:

- **Set Goals:** Use progress tracking to challenge yourself with "virtual hikes" or distance goals.

- **Multiplayer Options:** Some apps allow you to compete or workout with friends virtually.

- **Mix It Up:** Pair VR workouts with other activities to avoid overreliance on the tech.

Safety and Accessibility:

- **Clear Your Workout Space:** Avoid collisions by ensuring a safe, uncluttered workout area.

- **Gradual Intensity Increases:** Don't overexert yourself, even if the virtual world feels limitless.

- **Physician Consultation:** Check with your doctor if you have concerns about VR and exercise intensity.

Call to Action:

Ready to turn your workouts into epic adventures? Gear up and immerse yourself in the exciting world of VR Fitness!

18

Anti-Gravity Workouts

Take Your Workouts to New Heights: Experience Anti-Gravity Fitness

Brief Description:

DEFY GRAVITY AND REDISCOVER the joy of movement! Anti-gravity workouts use specialized technology, like air-pressurized treadmills or suspension harnesses, to reduce your body weight. This allows for high-intensity, low-impact exercise that's easier on joints, perfect for injury recovery, managing chronic pain, or adding a unique challenge.

Why It's Great for Retirees:

- **Joint-Friendly Fitness:** Drastically reduces impact on knees, hips, and ankles, promoting pain-free movement.

- **Post-Injury Rehabilitation:** A safe way to regain strength and mobility after surgery or injuries.

- **Break Through Plateaus:** Novel training stimulus can reignite fitness motivation and progress.

- **Feels Like a Kid Again:** The sensation of reduced weight can be liberating and playful.

Getting Started:

- **Locate Specialized Facilities:** Anti-gravity fitness is often found at rehab centers, sports performance facilities, or innovative gyms.

- **Introductory Sessions:** Book a session with a qualified trainer for proper instruction and safety overview.

- **Assess Your Comfort Level:** Start with shorter sessions and gradually increase intensity.

Resources Needed:

- **Anti-Gravity Facility Directory:** Search for centers near you that offer anti-gravity treadmills or other suspension systems.

- **Trainer Expertise:** Ensure instructors are knowledgeable about anti-gravity training and safety protocols.

- **Proper Attire:** Wear comfortable, form-fitting workout clothes to avoid tangling with equipment.

Challenges and Tips:

- **Availability and Cost:** Specialized facilities can be limited and sessions may be more expensive.

- **Initial Adjustment:** It takes time to get used to the sensation of reduced weight.

- **Don't Neglect Core Strength:** Stabilizing your body in anti-gravity still requires good core engagement.

Ways to Deepen the Experience:

- **Targeted Training:** Use anti-gravity for recovery runs, walking programs, or sport-specific drills.

- **Suspension Systems:** Explore anti-gravity yoga or bodyweight exercises using harnesses for added challenge.

- **Track Your Progress:** Notice improvements in joint pain, range of motion, or overall fitness.

Safety and Accessibility:

- **Supervised Sessions:** Especially important for those with balance concerns or health conditions.

- **Weight Restrictions:** Be aware of equipment limits and adjust pressure settings accordingly.

- **Communicate and Listen to Your Body:** Start slow and report any unusual discomfort.

Call to Action:

Ready to lighten the load and experience the unique benefits of anti-gravity exercise? Find a facility near you and prepare to take your workouts to the next level!

19

Fitness Flash Mobs

Get Fit and Get Noticed: Unleash the Power of Fitness Flash Mobs

Brief Description:

FORGET STUFFY GYMS! FITNESS Flash Mobs turn public spaces into impromptu workout parties. Join choreographed group workouts, lasting just a few energetic songs, for a burst of exercise, laughter, and pure fun. They're designed to inject a little healthy chaos into your day.

Why It's Great for Retirees:

- **Break the Routine:** Add a dose of spontaneity and excitement to your fitness routine.

- **Social and Uplifting:** The camaraderie of moving together with strangers creates an instant sense of connection.

- **Low-Commitment, High-Reward:** Short bursts of activity fit busy schedules and leave you energized.

- **Spread the Fitness Joy:** Inspire others to get moving!

Getting Started:

- **Find Your Flash Mob:** Search online groups like "Fitness Flash Mob [Your City]" or social media.

- **Rehearse a Little:** Organizers usually share the simple choreography ahead of time for practice.

- **Choose Your Spot:** Flash mobs often take over parks, plazas, or other open spaces.

Resources Needed:

- **Social Media Savvy:** Search for flash mob groups on Facebook, Instagram, or local community forums.

- **Portable Speaker:** Pump up the jams and get everyone in the fitness party mood.

- **Video Inspiration:** Watch existing fitness flash mob videos to get inspired and see the joyful mayhem!

Challenges and Tips:

- **Shyness Factor:** Let the energy of the crowd sweep you away – it's okay if you miss a few steps!

- **Location Permission:** Larger groups might need to check with local authorities for designated areas.

- **Respect Public Space:** Be mindful of other park users and try and choose open, less congested areas.

Ways to Deepen the Experience:

- **Theme It Up:** 80s aerobics attire, superhero costumes, anything goes for added fun!

- **Promote Your Cause:** Raise awareness for a healthy lifestyle or a charity with your flash mob.

- **Turn it into a Series:** Organize regular flash mobs at different locations to keep the momentum going.

Safety and Accessibility:

- **Choose Simple Choreography:** Inclusive for everyone, regardless of fitness level.

- **Hydration Stations:** Especially in warm weather, have water on hand for participants.

- **Warm-Up, Cool-Down:** Include these to prevent injuries and promote recovery.

Call to Action:

Ready to add a burst of unexpected energy and fun to your day? Find a Fitness Flash Mob near you and get ready to move!

20

Circus Skills Workshops

Step into the Spotlight: Discover the Joy of Circus Skills

Brief Description:

REDISCOVER PLAYFULNESS AND CHALLENGE yourself while learning the basics of juggling, tightrope walking, acrobatics, and more. In a fun and supportive environment, develop balance, strength, and coordination in a way that feels more like an adventure than exercise.

Why It's Great for Retirees:

- **Rediscover Your Inner Child:** Tap into a sense of playfulness and joy often lost in adulthood.

- **Challenge Yourself Safely:** Learn new skills in a structured setting with proper instruction and safety measures.

- **Novel Fitness Experience:** Break out of traditional gym routines with movements that feel both exciting and empowering.

- **Build Community:** Bond with others embracing a shared sense of fun and overcoming playful challenges.

Getting Started:

- **Skill Level Focus:** Emphasize that these workshops are beginner-friendly.

- **Supportive and Safe Atmosphere:** Instructors should prioritize a positive and fun environment for exploration.

- **Start with the Basics:** Focus on foundational juggling, balancing, and simple tumbling skills.

Resources Needed:

- **Workshop Spaces:** Community centers, gyms, or studios with enough space for safe movement.

- **Qualified Instructors:** Background in circus arts, gymnastics, or movement instruction is ideal.

- **Basic Props and Safety Equipment:** Juggling balls/pins, balance beams, soft mats, etc.

Challenges and Tips:

- **Fear Factor:** Promote a playful, non-judgmental space to encourage participation.

- **Individualized Progression:** Offer variations so everyone feels both challenged and successful.

- **Highlight the Fun of 'Failing':** Normalize trying new things and celebrate the process, not just the outcome.

Ways to Deepen the Experience:

- **Mini-Performances:** Host an informal showcase to celebrate progress and build a supportive community.

- **Collaboration:** Partner with dancers or theater groups for integrated skills workshops.

- **Explore Circus History:** Supplement workshops with talks or films on the rich history of circus arts.

Safety and Accessibility:

- **Proper Instruction:** Emphasize safe techniques for all skills being taught.

- **Modifications and Alternatives:** Offer options for different fitness levels and abilities.

- **Participant Awareness:** Encourage honesty about limitations and emphasize listening to one's body.

Call to Action:

Ready to unleash your inner acrobat and embrace a sense of playful challenge? Find a Circus Skills Workshop near you and step into the extraordinary!

Technology and Innovation

21

DIY Smart Home Gadgets

Take Control: Create Your Own Smart Home Devices

Brief Description:

DEMYSTIFY SMART HOME TECHNOLOGY and learn to build your own simple gadgets to automate tasks and add convenience to your life. Start with beginner-friendly projects and get hands-on with basic IoT kits and platforms.

Why It's Great for Retirees:

- **Boost Independence:** Create solutions that make everyday life easier and safer.

- **Empowering Skill Building:** Discover new abilities and keep your mind sharp with engaging tech projects.

- **No Tech Expertise Needed:** Workshops focus on guided learning with user-friendly platforms.

- **Cost-Effective Customization:** Tailor smart home solutions to your exact needs without buying expensive commercial products.

Getting Started

- **Focus on Simplicity:** Choose projects like smart lighting or automated plant watering for quick wins.

- **Easy to Use Platforms:** Opt for intuitive visual programming platforms (e.g., Node-RED, IFTTT).

- **Clear Step-by-Steps:** Provide detailed instructions and opportunities for guided troubleshooting.

Resources Needed:

- **Basic IoT Kits:** Options like Arduino or Raspberry Pi starter kits, along with simple sensors.

- **Workshop Leaders:** Those with IoT knowledge and a talent for making tech accessible.

- **Community Support:** Online forums or groups focused on the chosen platforms for continuing help.

Challenges and Tips

- **Tech Hesitation:** Start small and celebrate even minor successes to build confidence.

- **Troubleshooting Mindset:** Frame 'bugs' as puzzles to solve, promoting perseverance and problem-solving

- **The Jargon Barrier:** Explain technical terms in plain language.

Ways to Deepen the Experience

- **Real-World Applications:** Focus on projects with direct benefits to safety, energy saving, etc.

- **Partner with Makerspaces:** Access tools, expertise, and a collaborative environment.

- **Skill-Sharing Sessions:** Participants share their creations and knowledge to inspire each other.

Safety and Accessibility:

- **Electrical Safety:** Emphasize proper handling and use of basic components and wiring.

- **Accessible Instruction:** Accommodate different learning paces and offer visual aids/written instructions.

- **Online Support:** Provide resources for continued learning and connect participants with helpful forums.

Call to Action:

Ready to make your home work for you? Join a DIY Smart Home Gadgets workshop and turn your living space into a hub of personalized convenience!

22

Augmented Reality (AR) Scavenger Hunts

Explore Hidden Wonders: Augmented Reality Scavenger Hunts

Brief Description:

TURN YOUR SURROUNDINGS INTO a digital playground! AR scavenger hunts use your smartphone or tablet to reveal hidden clues, solve puzzles, and complete challenges in the real world. Explore local history, discover hidden art, or unravel a playful mystery.

Why It's Great for Retirees:

- **Combines Exploration and Tech:** Get outdoors while engaging with cutting-edge AR technology.

- **Mental and Physical Stimulation:** Keeps your mind sharp with puzzles and encourages movement.

- **Playful Learning:** Discover new things about your own city or neighborhood in a fun way.

- **Social Option:** Participate in team-based hunts for collaboration and a sense of friendly competition.

Getting Started:

- **Find or Create Hunts:** Search for existing AR scavenger hunts in your area or use platforms to build your own.

- **The Right Tools:** Ensure your device is AR-compatible and download any necessary apps.

- **Start Simple:** Begin with shorter hunts and easier puzzles to build understanding and confidence.

Resources Needed:

- **Local AR Experiences:** Search "[Your city] AR Scavenger Hunts" or use platforms like Niantic.

- **AR Development Apps:** For creating your own, try user-friendly options like Metaverse or BFIELD.

- **Community Collaboration:** Partner with tech-savvy teens or local groups for design help.

Challenges and Tips:

- **Tech Glitches:** Have backup plans (paper clues) and test hunts thoroughly beforehand.

- **Accessibility:** Design routes with varying distances and wheelchair-friendly options.

- **Varying the Theme:** Keep it fresh with historical, artistic, or seasonal scavenger hunts.

Ways to Deepen the Experience:

- **Story-Driven Hunts:** Create a narrative around your clues to add a layer of mystery or adventure.

- **Local Lore:** Incorporate hidden local history and trivia for a unique learning experience.

- **Partnership Potential:** Collaborate with museums or businesses to design themed hunts.

Safety and Accessibility:

- **Awareness of Surroundings:** Encourage participants to be mindful of traffic and avoid unsafe areas.

- **Weather Preparedness:** Suggest appropriate gear and provide contingency plans for bad weather.

- **Options for All:** Offer variations in difficulty and physical exertion to be inclusive.

Call to Action:

Ready to transform your world into an interactive adventure? Search for AR Scavenger Hunts near you or get creative designing your own!

23

Blockchain and Cryptocurrency Club

Decoding Crypto: Join the Blockchain and Cryptocurrency Club

Brief Description:

CUT THROUGH THE BUZZWORDS and gain a solid understanding of blockchain technology, cryptocurrencies like Bitcoin, and the potential impact on our financial future. Explore safe investment strategies, learn about crypto mining, and discover practical uses for digital currencies.

Why It's Great for Retirees:

- **Manage Financial Change:** Learn how crypto could disrupt traditional banking and investing.

- **Protect Against Scams:** Gain the knowledge to spot risks and make informed decisions.

- **Potential Income Source:** Explore mining and investing, with a focus on responsible strategies.

- **Stimulating Learning:** Embrace a new, complex topic that keeps your mind sharp.

Getting Started:

- **Beginner-Focused:** Emphasize that no prior knowledge is required.

- **Plain Language:** Explain technical terms clearly and avoid overwhelming jargon.

- **Reputable Sources:** Focus on trusted resources and educators within the crypto space.

Resources Needed:

- **Local Groups or Classes:** Check community centers, libraries, or online learning platforms.

- **Credible Crypto News Sites:** Sources like CoinDesk or Cointelegraph for unbiased updates.

- **Safety-First Communities:** Online forums with a focus on education and risk assessment.

Challenges and Tips:

- **The Volatility Factor:** Discuss the risks alongside potential rewards of cryptocurrency investment.

- **"Get Rich Quick" Mentality:** Promote a long-term perspective and responsible participation.

- **Staying Current:** The crypto landscape changes rapidly, so emphasize ongoing learning.

Ways to Deepen the Experience:

- **Guest Speakers:** Invite experts on crypto regulation, taxation, or specific investment strategies.

- **"Practice" Wallets:** Use simulated environments to explore buying/selling without real money.

- **Focus on Practical Applications:** Discuss how crypto is used for payments, remittances, etc.

Safety and Accessibility:

- **Prioritize Security:** Teach best practices for storing crypto and avoiding online scams.

- **Beware of Hype:** Encourage a critical eye toward overly promotional projects or influencers.

- **Financial Risk Awareness:** Stress that crypto is a new asset class and only invest disposable income.

Call to Action:

- Ready to navigate the exciting and complex world of crypto? Join a Blockchain and Cryptocurrency Club and empower yourself with knowledge!

24

3D Printing Masterclasses

Master the Future of Creation: 3D Printing Masterclasses

Brief Description:

UNLOCK THE WORLD OF 3D printing! Learn to design your own 3D models using user-friendly software and bring them to life with 3D printers. Explore the amazing possibilities of this technology to create everything from customized jewelry to replacement parts to medical prosthetics.

Why It's Great for Retirees:

- **Express Your Creativity:** Turn your ideas into tangible objects, whether artistic or functional.

- **Practical Problem-Solving:** Design solutions to everyday challenges with custom-printed tools.

- **Tap into Tech Innovation:** Be part of the cutting-edge "maker movement" and its potential impact.

- **Entrepreneurial Potential:** Explore selling your 3D printed creations or offering print services.

Getting Started:

- **Focus on User-Friendliness:** Use CAD software designed for beginners, like Tinkercad or SketchUp.

- **Access to Printers:** Check for classes at makerspaces, libraries, or educational centers.

- **Start with Small Projects:** Build confidence with simple designs before tackling complex creations.

Resources Needed:

- **Community Hubs:** Search for local makerspaces or 3D printing workshops in your area.

- **Beginner-friendly Tutorials:** 3D printing websites and YouTube channels offer clear instructions.

- **Printable Model Libraries:** Websites like Thingiverse offer pre-made designs to modify and print.

Challenges and Tips:

- **The Learning Curve:** Expect some trial and error as you master design software and printer settings.

- **Realistic Expectations:** Highlight both the amazing capabilities and limitations of 3D printing.

- **Troubleshooting Mindset:** Frame errors as opportunities to learn and refine your process.

Ways to Deepen the Experience:

- **Specialized Skills:** Offer workshops on 3D printing for jewelry, miniatures, or assistive devices.

- **Collaboration Opportunities:** Partner with artists or engineers to showcase diverse applications.

- **3D Print Showcases:** Organize an exhibit of participant creations to inspire and share knowledge.

Safety and Accessibility:

- **Proper Ventilation:** Ensure good airflow when using certain types of 3D printers and materials.

- **Material Safety:** Provide guidance on choosing non-toxic and safe filaments.

- **Instruction for All:** Offer adaptive tools and techniques for those with limited dexterity.

Call to Action:

Ready to turn your imagination into reality? Sign up for a 3D Printing Masterclass and discover the wonders of additive manufacturing!

25

Robotics Challenges for Adults

Build, Program, Compete: Join the Fun of Robotics Challenges

Brief Description:

PUT YOUR PROBLEM-SOLVING SKILLS and creativity to the test by designing and programming robots to tackle a variety of challenges. Work as part of a team or individually, learning the basics of robotics, coding, and engineering in an engaging, competitive environment.

Why It's Great for Retirees:

- **Lifelong Learning:** Embrace hands-on STEM (Science, Technology, Engineering, Math) challenges.

- **Teamwork and Collaboration:** Work together to brainstorm, build, and troubleshoot robot designs.

- **Playful Problem-solving:** Apply logical thinking and creativity to overcome obstacles.

- **Rediscover the Joy of Building:** Experience the satisfaction of creating something functional and exciting.

Getting Started:

- **Find Your Challenge:** Search for local or online robotics competitions with beginner-friendly options.

- **Choose Your Kit:** Competitions may provide them, or pick a user-friendly robotics kit (e.g., Lego Mindstorms).

- **No Experience Needed:** Many challenges emphasize learning and collaboration over prior expertise.

Resources Needed:

- **Robotics Competition Listings:** Search for adult-focused challenges or those with tiered difficulty levels.

- **Makerspaces and Community Tech Hubs:** May offer equipment, classes, and collaborative spaces.

- **Beginner Robotics Resources:** Books, tutorials on simple platforms like Arduino or Raspberry Pi.

Challenges and Tips:

- **Embrace Failure as Learning:** Robotics involves debugging! Frame setbacks as part of the process.

- **Ask for Help:** Competitions usually offer mentorship and resources to support learners.

- **Celebrate Every Step:** Acknowledge progress in design, coding, even when the robot isn't perfect yet!

Ways to Deepen the Experience:

- **Theme-Based Challenges:** Robots that navigate mazes, sort objects, or even play a simple sport.

- **Showcase Events:** Host a "robot show-and-tell" for participants to share their creations and strategies.

- **Mentorship Program:** Connect experienced roboticists with beginners for guidance and support.

Safety and Accessibility:

- **Tool Training:** Provide instruction in safe use of any soldering or cutting tools required.

- **Adaptive Options:** Ensure challenges can be modified for participants with varying abilities.

- **Team Formation Assistance:** Help connect solo learners with teams to foster collaboration.

Call to Action:

Ready to unleash your inner engineer and experience the excitement of robotics? Seek out a Robotics Challenge and discover what you and your robot can achieve!

26

ElderTech Innovation Lab

Solving Real-World Challenges: Join the ElderTech Innovation Lab

Brief Description:

THIS COLLABORATIVE SPACE INVITES retirees to apply their life experience, skills, and creativity to develop new technologies that address the specific needs and challenges faced by older adults. Partner with engineers, designers, and entrepreneurs to brainstorm, prototype, and potentially bring your tech solutions to life.

Why It's Great for Retirees:

- **Make a Meaningful Impact:** Harness your wisdom to improve the lives of yourself and your peers.

- **Contribute Your Unique Skills:** Share your knowledge from diverse backgrounds and professions.

- **Creative Collaboration:** Work alongside a dynamic intergenerational team driven by a shared purpose.

- **Lifelong Learning:** Explore new fields like human-centered design and assistive technology.

Getting Started:

- **Find Your Lab:** Seek out ElderTech incubators or innovation hubs affiliated with universities or companies.

- **Openness to the Process:** Be willing to contribute ideas, test prototypes, and refine concepts.

- **No Tech Background Required:** Your life experience and problem-solving insights are invaluable.

Resources Needed:

- **University Partnerships:** Many universities have innovation labs that welcome community involvement.

- **ElderTech Organizations:** Check out nonprofits like AARP's innovation programs for potential connections.

- **Online Communities:** Groups focused on ElderTech or assistive technology can guide your search.

Challenges and Tips:

- **Finding the Right Fit:** Not all labs operate the same, so ask about their focus and participation process.

- **Team Dynamics:** Embrace working with people of all ages and backgrounds, valuing diverse input.

- **The Long Game:** Tech development takes time – be patient with the iterative design and testing process.

Ways to Deepen the Experience:

- **Problem-Specific Focus:** Labs could specialize in areas like mobility, health tracking, or social connection.

- **'Tech Tester' Programs:** Create a feedback loop of retirees providing insights on early prototypes.

- **Showcase and Pitch Events:** Host events to connect ElderTech innovators with potential investors.

Safety and Accessibility:

- **Inclusive Environment:** Ensure the lab space and activities are accessible for varying abilities.

- **Respect for Experience:** Foster a culture where everyone feels valued, regardless of tech background.

- **Ethics and Privacy:** Prioritize responsible technology development that prioritizes user safety.

Call to Action:

Ready to use your skills and experience to shape the future of aging? Find an ElderTech Innovation Lab and join a team making a real difference!

27

Virtual Reality (VR) World Building

Become an Architect of Virtual Worlds: Discover VR World Building

Brief Description:

DIVE INTO THE EXTRAORDINARY world of VR design! Learn to use powerful VR world-building software to craft immersive environments, design interactive experiences, and tell stories in new and exciting ways. No prior experience is required.

Why It's Great for Retirees:

- **Tap Into Limitless Creativity:** VR offers a canvas where imagination is your only boundary.

- **Explore Without Leaving Home:** Build breathtaking landscapes, fantastical cities, or cozy rooms all from the comfort of home.

- **Empowering New Skills:** Learn cutting-edge VR design tools and feel at home in the digital realm.

- **A New Form of Storytelling:** Experiment with interactive narratives and games set within your own VR worlds.

Getting Started

- **Focus on User-Friendliness:** Choose world-building software designed for non-coders (Horizon Worlds, Mozilla Hubs, etc.).

- **Start Simple:** Emphasize mastering the basics of environment design, object placement, lighting, etc.

- **Provide a VR Headset:** If possible, offer accessible headsets for participants to experience their creations.

Resources Needed

- **Workshop Locations:** Seek out VR labs, makerspaces, or libraries that might offer equipment and space.

- **VR World-Building Software:** Research beginner-friendly options both free and paid.

- **Online Tutorials and Communities:** Supplement learning with online guides and supportive forums.

Challenges and Tips

- **Motion Sickness Potential:** Introduce VR gradually, offer seated experiences, and encourage breaks.

- **The Learning Curve:** Start with simple environments and prioritize small successes to build confidence.

- **"Just Playing" vs. Building:** Guide participants to have a goal (a simple maze, themed scene) rather than just exploration.

Ways to Deepen the Experience:

- **Collaborative Projects:** Teams could build interconnected VR worlds or contribute to a shared scene.

- **Focus on Storytelling:** Design VR spaces that evoke moods, tell a non-linear story, or guide the user.

- **Showcase and Feedback:** Host a "VR gallery walk" where participants experience each other's creations.

Safety and Accessibility:

- **Seizure Warnings:** Advise those with photo-sensitivity about potential flashing imagery in VR.

- **Virtual Obstacles:** Ensure designs have clear pathways so users don't bump into real-world objects.

- **Seated and Standing Options:** Offer variations for those with limited mobility.

Call to Action:

Ready to unleash your inner architect and bring your virtual dreams to life? Find a VR World Building workshop and step into a realm of limitless imagination!

28

Tech-Savvy Traveling

Tech-Savvy Traveling: Seminars for the Modern Explorer

Brief Description:

THIS SEMINAR SERIES EQUIPS you with the tech tools to become a more confident and informed traveler. Learn how to navigate unfamiliar cities with ease, overcome language barriers, and discover hidden gems using a variety of user-friendly apps and online resources.

Why It's Great for Retirees:

- **Travel with Confidence:** Mastering essential travel apps empowers you to explore independently.

- **Embrace New Technology:** Learn valuable tech skills that can be applied beyond travel.

- **Uncover Hidden Gems:** Go beyond tourist traps and discover unique experiences curated by your interests.

- **Connect with Locals:** Language translation apps bridge communication gaps and foster cultural exchange.

Seminar Topics:

- **Navigation Essentials:** Mastering mapping apps (Google Maps, Citymapper) for public transport, walking routes, and offline access.

- **Translation Power:** Utilizing translation apps (Google Translate, Reverso) for menus, conversations, and navigating signs.

- **Finding Hidden Gems:** Exploring apps like TripAdvisor, Airbnb Experiences, and local event listings to discover unique attractions beyond the usual tourist spots.

- **Staying Connected:** Using apps like WhatsApp, Viber, and Skype for cost-effective communication with loved ones back home.

- **Travel Safety Apps:** Showcasing emergency translation apps, offline medical dictionaries, and local safety resources.

Getting Started:

- **Focus on User-Friendliness:** Prioritize apps with large icons, clear interfaces, and voice-activated options.

- **Practice Makes Perfect:** Encourage participants to download and explore the apps beforehand.

- **Offer Hands-on Training:** Dedicate time within the seminar for personalized guidance on app usage.

Resources Needed:

- **Tech-Savvy Instructors:** Seek facilitators comfortable with travel apps and explaining them in a clear, step-by-step manner.

- **Smart Device Lab:** If feasible, have a space with tablets or smartphones pre-loaded with relevant apps for practice.

- **Printable Resources:** Provide one-pagers with app recommendations, tutorials, and cheat sheets for common travel situations.

Challenges and Tips:

- **Tech Anxiety:** Address concerns patiently, emphasize the user-friendly nature of the apps.

- **Limited Data Availability:** Discuss offline functionalities of apps and strategies for Wi-Fi access abroad.

- **Varying Tech Comfort Levels:** Offer tiered sessions for beginners, intermediate, and advanced users.

Ways to Deepen the Experience:

- **Guest Speakers:** Invite travel bloggers or vloggers who leverage technology to share their experiences.

- **Post-Seminar Travel Groups:** Facilitate connections between participants for future group trips utilizing their newfound tech skills.

- **"Tech Travel Challenges":** Set playful challenges (finding the best local restaurant using an app) to reinforce learning.

Safety and Accessibility:

- **Data Security Tips:** Educate participants on using secure Wi-Fi networks and avoiding scams.

- **Accessibility Features:** Highlight accessibility features built into apps for visually impaired or mobility-challenged users.

- **Alternatives for Non-Smartphone Users:** Suggest travel guides and offline resources for those who prefer non-digital methods.

Call to Action:

Ready to ditch the bulky guidebooks and embrace the power of travel apps? Sign up for a Tech-Savvy Traveling seminar and unlock a world of exploration possibilities!

29

Gaming and Coding Bootcamps

Gaming and Coding Bootcamps: Create Your Own Games, Unlock Your Tech Skills

Brief Description:

EVER WANTED TO MAKE your own video game? Our bootcamps offer a fun and interactive way to learn coding by building simple games from scratch. Master programming fundamentals, unleash your creativity, and gain tech skills that empower you to bring your game ideas to life.

Why It's Great for Retirees:

- **Learning Through Play:** Discover coding concepts easily and intuitively through a game-making framework.

- **No Experience Needed** Our bootcamps are beginner-friendly, welcoming those with zero coding knowledge.

- **Rediscover Problem-Solving:** Develop logical thinking and problem-solving skills in an engaging format.

- **Unlock a New World:** Demystify tech and gain a sense of accomplishment as you build working games.

Getting Started:

- **Bootcamp Focus:** Choose based on desired game style (puzzle, platformers, retro arcade, etc.)

- **Programming Language:** Intro-friendly options like Scratch, Python, or specifically designed for game development.

- **Structured Guidance:** Effective bootcamps provide step-by-step instruction and ongoing support.

Resources Needed:

- **Computer Access:** Bootcamps may have computer labs or require participants to bring their own laptops.

- **Software:** Instructors should provide any necessary coding tools or game development software.

- **Patience and Creativity:** Building even a simple game takes time, but the reward is in the journey.

Challenges and Tips:

- **Tackling Tech Jargon:** Instructors should clearly explain terminology in a non-intimidating way.

- **Bite-Sized Projects:** Focus on small, achievable game builds to maintain a sense of progress.

- **Celebrating Small Wins:** Showcase student-created games to foster camaraderie and pride in their work.

Ways to Deepen the Experience:

- **Modding Option:** Learn to modify existing games as a stepping stone to creating your own totally original ones.

- **Game Design Exploration:** Discuss game mechanics, level design, and storytelling within games.

- **Collaborative Projects:** Allow for teams to work together on larger game concepts.

Safety and Accessibility:

- **Pace and Breaks:** Build in time for questions and address technical hiccups without rushing.

- **Supportive Environment:** Emphasize the joy of learning, not competition or comparison.

- **Diverse Instructors:** Representation matters! Creates a more welcoming environment for all learners.

Call to Action:

Ready to unleash your inner game designer? Explore Gaming and Coding Bootcamps and see what incredible creations you'll bring to life!

30

Digital Music Creation

Unleash Your Inner Composer: Explore Digital Music Creation

Brief Description:

DISCOVER THE POWER OF creating music at your fingertips. Learn how to use intuitive music software to craft your own beats, melodies, and even full compositions. Explore your musical side, have fun, and bring your musical ideas to life, regardless of experience level.

Why It's Great for Retirees:

- **Rediscover Your Musicality:** Explore your creativity, even if you never played an instrument before.

- **Technology as a Creative Tool:** Learn that tech can be an instrument for musical expression.

- **No Experience Required:** Modern software makes music creation accessible and fun for beginners.

- **Stress Relief and Joy:** The act of creating music is both relaxing and creatively stimulating.

Getting Started:

- **Software Options:** Focus on user-friendly DAWs (Digital Audio Workstations) like GarageBand, Audacity, or Soundtrap.

- **MIDI Controllers (Optional):** Simple keyboards can enhance the experience but aren't essential.

- **Sample Libraries:** Provide a starting point for sounds and inspiration to build from.

Resources Needed:

- **Workshop Spaces:** Computer labs, music studios, or spaces suitable for listening with headphones/speakers.

- **Knowledgeable Instructors:** Background in music production and teaching technology to beginners is ideal.

- **Online Resources:** Supplement workshops with tutorials and communities specific to your chosen software.

Challenges and Tips:

- **Busting the "Musician" Myth:** You don't need to read music or have played instruments to get started.

- **Experimentation is Key:** Encourage playfulness over striving for perfection early on.

- **Build Confidence Gradually:** Start with simple loops and adding layers instead of full compositions.

Ways to Deepen the Experience:

- **Genre Exploration:** Sessions focused on electronic music, hip-hop beats, or soundtrack-style music.

- **Songwriting Integration:** Incorporate lyrics and basic vocal recording for a full creative process.

- **Collaborative Jams:** Participants can work together to make a layered piece, combining their unique sounds.

Safety and Accessibility:

- **Headphone Awareness:** Encourage breaks and safe volume levels for workshops involving headphones.

- **Adaptive Options:** Explore accessibility features in software and potential for adapted MIDI controllers.

- **Supportive Environment:** Emphasize that it's about personal expression not competing for musical mastery.

Call to Action:

Ready to awaken your inner musician? Dive into a Digital Music Creation workshop and experience the joy of turning your ideas into sound!

31

Start a family history podcast

Become a Family Historian: Start a Legacy Podcast

Brief Description:

PRESERVE PRICELESS FAMILY STORIES and create a time capsule for future generations by launching your very own family history podcast. Learn simple interviewing techniques, recording basics, and how to share your episodes with loved ones.

Why It's Great for Retirees:

- **Meaningful Project:** Dive deep into your family's past, uncovering hidden stories and connecting the dots of your lineage.

- **Technology as a Tool:** Embrace easy-to-use platforms to record, edit, and share your podcast with ease.

- **Strengthening Bonds:** Foster deeper connections with relatives as they share memories, and engage younger generations as listeners.

- **Legacy Building:** Leave a priceless gift for future generations, ensuring family voices and stories live on.

Getting Started:

- **Interview Prep:** Craft open-ended questions that spark vivid memories and storytelling.

- **Choosing Your Tech:** Explore free recording apps on your phone or tablet, or invest in simple podcasting gear.

- **Platform Matters:** Opt for user-friendly hosting sites to easily share your finished podcast episodes with family.

Resources Needed:

- **Smartphone or Tablet:** Most have built-in microphones sufficient for casual recording.

- **Quiet Space:** Minimize background noise for clear recordings.

- **List of Questions:** Prepare a starting point for your interviews to focus the conversation.

Challenges and Tips:

- **Start with Willing Relatives:** Begin with those enthusiastic about sharing their stories.

- **Editing Basics:** Learn simple audio editing software to trim pauses or add intros.

- **Keep it Casual:** Natural conversations are often the most engaging for listeners.

Ways to Deepen the Experience:

- **Theme Each Episode:** Focus on specific events, time periods, or family branches per episode.

- **Incorporate Music:** Add old family favorites or era-appropriate tunes for atmosphere.

- **"Young Voices" Segment:** Interview children or teens in the family for a modern-day counterpoint.

Call to Action:

Don't let your family's stories fade with time. Start planning your first podcast episode today and preserve your unique family legacy!

Volunteering and Community Service

32

Eco-Warrior Expeditions

Become an Eco-Warrior: Join Hands-On Environmental Expeditions

Brief Description:

GET ACTIVE IN THE fight for a healthier planet! Eco-Warrior Expeditions offer volunteer opportunities focused on hands-on conservation work. Contribute to reforestation projects, assist with wildlife conservation efforts, participate in clean-up campaigns in beautiful but vulnerable natural areas, and make a tangible difference.

Why It's Great for Retirees:

- **Combine Travel with Purpose:** Experience new places while actively contributing to their ecological health.

- **Meaningful Impact:** See the direct, positive results of your efforts on the environment.

- **Outdoor Activity with a Cause:** Enjoy physical work (to your ability) in stunning natural settings.

- **Connect with Like-Minded People:** Build community with others passionate about the environment.

Getting Started:

- **Diverse Opportunities:** Seek expeditions offering varied physical demands and skill requirements.

- **Trip Lengths:** Choose between short weekend projects or longer immersive conservation experiences.

- **Physical Considerations:** Be honest about your fitness level and seek projects that match it.

Resources Needed:

- **Expedition Providers:** Research reputable organizations like Earthwatch, Sierra Club, or local conservation groups.

- **Expedition-Specific Information:** Detailed overviews of activities, accommodations, and required gear.

- **Participant Reviews:** Seek feedback from past participants, especially those of similar age and ability.

Challenges and Tips:

- **Physical Demands:** Choose expeditions honestly aligned with your fitness level (you can build up!).

- **Cost Factor:** Some expeditions may be a financial investment – factor this into your decision.

- **"Eco-Tourism" Caution:** Ensure the organization prioritizes conservation, not just the volunteer experience.

Ways to Deepen the Experience:

- **Focused Skill-Building:** Some expeditions offer training in wildlife tracking, ecological surveying, etc.

- **Local Connection:** Projects that collaborate with local communities for sustainable conservation efforts.

- **Post-Expedition Action:** Learn how to continue your eco efforts even after returning home.

Safety and Accessibility:

- **Thorough Trip Descriptions:** Ensure accommodations and activities are suitable for your needs.

- **Group Leaders and Support:** Expeditions should have trained leaders and emergency protocols.

- **Open Communication:** Discuss any health considerations or mobility limitations with the organizers.

Call to Action:

Ready to roll up your sleeves and fight for our planet? Search for Eco-Warrior Expeditions and unleash your inner environmental champion!

33

Tech Tutoring for Seniors

Empowering Seniors: Become a Tech Tutor and Share Your Skills

Brief Description:

Do you enjoy helping others and have some tech savvy? Turn your digital know-how into a force for good! Volunteer as a Tech Tutor, offering personalized, patient guidance to help other seniors navigate smartphones, computers, tablets, and the online world with confidence.

Why It's Great for Retirees:

- **Make a Meaningful Impact:** Bridge the digital divide and empower seniors with vital skills.

- **Share Your Passion:** If you love tech, spread that enthusiasm in a supportive setting.

- **Mental Stimulation:** Explaining tech concepts helps keep your own skills sharp.

- **Build Community:** Develop friendships and a sense of purpose through the tutoring process.

Getting Started:

- **Volunteer Opportunities:** Libraries, senior centers, or community groups often need tech tutors.

- **Tailor Your Skills:** Be clear about your areas of expertise (email, social media, device basics, etc.).

- **Patience is Key:** Be prepared to go slowly, repeat concepts, and celebrate every small success.

Resources Needed:

- **Local Programs:** Search for "[Your Area] Senior Tech Tutoring" or inquire at community centers.

- **Teaching Materials:** Simple handouts, cheat sheets, or online tutorials can supplement your explanations.

- **Senior-Focused Tech Resources:** Websites like SeniorNet offer helpful guides written specifically for older learners.

Challenges and Tips:

- **Fear and Frustration:** Reassure learners that everyone struggles at first & frame mistakes as learning opportunities.

- **Jargon Jungle:** Explain technical terms in plain language using everyday analogies.

- **Varied Learning Styles:** Be prepared to demonstrate, use visuals, and let them try things hands-on.

Ways to Deepen the Experience:

- **One-on-One vs. Small Groups:** Offer options depending on the learner's comfort level.

- **"Reverse Mentoring":** Have seniors share their life experience for a sense of exchange, not just instruction.

- **Beyond the Basics:** Offer guidance on setting up video calls, online hobbies, or safely using shopping apps.

Safety and Accessibility:

- **Online Safety Emphasis:** Cover password security, scams, and responsible social media use.

- **Physical Considerations:** Ensure adequate workspace lighting, good seating, and break times.

- **Respect and Empathy:** Foster a trusting environment where seniors feel comfortable asking 'silly' questions.

Call to Action:

Ready to share your digital skills and empower your peers? Seek out Tech Tutoring opportunities in your community and make a difference!

34

Cultural Exchange Programs

Expand Your Horizons: Discover the Power of Cultural Exchange

Brief Description:

IMMERSE YOURSELF IN A different culture and build bridges of understanding through enriching exchange programs. Options range from volunteer exchanges, where you offer skills while living abroad, to structured programs focused on language immersion, cultural exploration, or intergenerational connection.

Why It's Great for Retirees:

- **Lifelong Learning in Action:** Experience a culture firsthand, beyond what any travel guide can offer.

- **Challenge Comfort Zones:** Embrace new ways of living, expanding your perspective.

- **Purposeful Travel:** Contribute your skills or time while connecting with locals on a deeper level.

- **Rediscover Your Adaptability:** Thrive in new environments, proving age is no barrier to adventure.

Getting Started:

- **Program Types:** Research volunteer exchanges, language study programs, or homestays with cultural focus.

- **Duration and Commitment:** Choose options from short-term to extended stays, depending on your availability.

- **Your Skills and Interests:** Seek programs that either utilize your expertise or let you learn something new!

Resources Needed:

- **Reputable Exchange Organizations:** Look for those with good reviews, safety standards, and support structures (like SERVAS, Cross-Cultural Solutions).

- **Cultural Preparation:** Organizations may offer resources, or supplement this with online research and language basics.

- **Open-Minded Community:** Seek programs catering to adults with a desire for meaningful interaction.

Challenges and Tips:

- **Stepping Outside the Familiar:** Culture shock is normal! Embrace the discomfort as part of growth.

- **Language Barriers:** Some language basics are helpful, but emphasize willingness to learn and non-verbal communication.

- **'Helping' vs. Imposing:** Approach your role as a learner and collaborator, not someone offering 'better' solutions.

Ways to Deepen the Experience:

- **Homestay Exchange:** Living with a local family offers unparalleled opportunities for immersion.

- **Intergenerational Programs:** Pair with student groups or young families for unique cross-cultural learning.

- **Shared Skill Projects:** Teach your craft while learning theirs – cooking, gardening, etc. – creating a bond.

Safety and Accessibility:

- **Organization Support:** Choose programs with emergency contacts and protocols.

- **Accommodation Awareness:** Ensure the living situation aligns with your needs and comfort level.

- **Health Considerations:** Discuss any health matters with the program and ensure access to necessary care.

Call to Action:

Ready to broaden your perspective and leave a positive mark on the world? Explore Cultural Exchange Programs and step into a truly transformative adventure!

35

Community Art Projects

Leave Your Mark: Contribute to Community Art Projects

Brief Description:

GET INVOLVED IN ADDING a splash of color, creative expression, and a sense of shared ownership to your community. Join or initiate projects that create murals, sculptures, community gardens, or other art installations that enhance public spaces.

Why It's Great for Retirees:

- **Share Creative Talents:** Utilize your artistic skills (or a willingness to learn!) for the greater good.

- **Connect Through Collaboration:** Work alongside a diverse group of people towards a shared creative vision.

- **Tangible Legacy:** See your efforts transform a space and contribute to a lasting sense of community pride.

- **Playful and Purposeful:** Enjoy the process of creating, regardless of the scale of your contribution.

Getting Started:

- **Find Your Project:** Look for existing initiatives at community centers, parks, or through local art groups.

- **Offer Your Skills:** Be it painting, design, gardening, or simply enthusiasm as a helping hand.

- **Be Part of the Process:** Some projects involve community input for design ideas, fostering ownership.

Resources Needed:

- **Community Hubs:** Libraries, community centers, or local art organizations often act as focal points.

- **Funding and Supplies:** Some projects have established funding, others may involve fundraising efforts.

- **Artist Leadership or Mentorship:** Ensure there's artistic guidance or access to learn needed skills.

Challenges and Tips:

- **Public Canvas = Varied Opinions:** Embrace differing perspectives and see compromise as part of collaboration.

- **Weather the Elements:** Choose project materials that stand up to the outdoors and plan workdays accordingly.

- **Maintenance Matters:** Projects may need upkeep, so consider a long-term care plan.

Ways to Deepen the Experience:

- **Tell a Story:** Let murals depict local history, or sculptures be inspired by community values.

- **Focus on Inclusion:** Projects intentionally designed for people with a range of abilities to participate.

- **Celebrate the Journey:** Host work-in-progress events to engage the wider community.

Safety and Accessibility:

- **Safe Work Environment:** Ensure proper tools, scaffolding, etc. and training if needed.

- **All Abilities Welcome:** Offer varying tasks or design elements accessible to diverse participants.

- **Respectful of Existing Spaces:** Community input is vital, ensuring the project enhances, not disrupts.

Call to Action:

Ready to add your creative touch to your community? Look for Community Art Projects or even plant the seed for a new one!

36

Historical Preservation Volunteers

Become a Guardian of the Past: Join Historical Preservation Efforts

Brief Description:

IMMERSE YOURSELF IN THE rich tapestry of your community's past! Volunteer on hands-on projects preserving historical buildings, digitizing archives, collecting oral histories, or contributing to educational exhibits that share local stories with future generations.

Why It's Great for Retirees:

- **Share Love of History:** Put your passion for the past to good use and learn even more in the process.

- **Diverse Opportunities to Suit Skills** Archivists, handy folks, interviewers – many talents are needed!

- **Sense of Legacy:** Help ensure local stories and landmarks are preserved for future generations.

- **Build Community with Fellow Buffs:** Connect with others who share your passion for the local history.

Getting Started:

- **Local is Best:** Historical societies, museums, preservation groups – focus on your community.

- **Your Skills + Their Needs:** Be upfront about your interests or skills so you're matched with a suitable project.

- **Commitment Level:** Clarify the time commitment, some projects may be ongoing, others task-specific.

Resources Needed:

- **Historical Organizations:** Search "[Your Area] Historical Society" or inquire at libraries/museums.

- **Volunteer Matching Websites:** Platforms like VolunteerMatch often list preservation opportunities.

- **Training and Support:** Larger projects may provide training or have mentors for specific tasks.

Challenges and Tips:

- **The Nitty-Gritty:** Some work may be detailed (archiving) or physically demanding (restoration).

- **Patience Required:** Preservation is painstaking – enjoy the process of uncovering and safeguarding the past.

- **Learn as You Go:** Even if you're not a history expert, organizations value enthusiasm and effort.

Ways to Deepen the Experience:

- **Oral History Projects:** Interview older residents, capturing voices and stories otherwise lost to time.

- **"History Detectives":** Research the origins of a building, artifact, or tradition, feeling like an investigator.

- **Historical Reenactment Tie-Ins:** Some groups collaborate, adding a performative element to their work.

Safety and Accessibility:

- **Varied Tasks = Varied Abilities:** Choose projects fitting your physical ability and mobility.

- **Respectful Handling:** Training in handling delicate artifacts or documents is often provided.

- **Team Environment:** Ensure the organization is welcoming and fosters a sense of shared purpose.

Call to Action:

Ready to play an active role in preserving the past? Discover Historical Preservation volunteer opportunities near you and leave your mark on the future!

37

Skill-Based Disaster Relief

Tap into Your Expertise: Skill-Based Disaster Relief

Brief Description:

DISASTERS CREATE URGENT NEEDS that retirees with specialized skills are uniquely positioned to fill. From engineers aiding in rebuilding to medical professionals offering care to counselors providing support, your experience can be invaluable in the aftermath of a crisis.

Why It's Great for Retirees:

- **Give Back in a Meaningful Way:** Channel your professional knowledge to make a tangible difference.

- **Your Skills are Needed:** Disasters often overwhelm local resources, creating a demand for your expertise.

- **Camaraderie and Purpose:** Work alongside a driven team, fostering a sense of shared mission.

- **Utilize Your Experience:** Your honed skills and problem-solving mindset are vital in chaotic situations.

Getting Started:

- **Disaster-Focused Organizations:** Red Cross, Habitat for Humanity, or specialized groups based on your skillset may offer deployment.

- **Be Realistic About Deployment:** Some involve travel to the affected area, others are remote support.

- **Time Commitments:** Varies greatly – from short-term relief missions to ongoing needs assessment.

Resources Needed:

- **Reputable Deployment Organizations:** Research their safety protocols, training, and support for volunteers.

- **Specialty Licenses/Certifications:** Ensure yours are current and understood by the organization.

- **Volunteer Community:** Connect with others who have deployed, both for advice and potential connections.

Challenges and Tips:

- **Crisis Environments:** Be prepared for high stress, difficult conditions, and potential emotional impact.

- **Matching Skills to Needs:** Being flexible helps, your first choice of deployment may not be available.

- **Age is NOT a Barrier, But:** Be honest about your physical capabilities for deployment on the ground.

Ways to Deepen the Experience:

- **Long-term Planning and Training:** Some groups offer readiness training for specific disaster roles.

- **Teach-back Opportunities:** Share your knowledge to train local responders, creating lasting impact.

- **Mental Health Awareness:** Proactive focus on self-care and debriefing is vital in this work.

Safety and Accessibility:

- **Deployment vs. Support:** Balance a desire to be on-site with the reality of physical demands. Remote help is also crucial.

- **Organization's Responsibility:** Understand your coverage (health, liability) and their emergency procedures.

- **Team Mentality:** You should never be deployed alone, ensuring well-being is everyone's responsibility.

Call to Action:

Ready to put your skills to work during the most challenging times? Explore Skill-Based Disaster Relief options and discover how to mobilize your experience for good!

38

Mentoring Startups

From Seasoned Pro to Startup Advisor: Become a Mentor

Brief Description:

SHARE YOUR KNOWLEDGE AND experience to guide young entrepreneurs as they navigate the thrilling, often turbulent, world of startups. Offer insights on strategy, financial planning, marketing, or draw upon your industry-specific expertise to help early-stage ventures succeed.

Why It's Great for Retirees:

- **Imparting Wisdom:** Pass on hard-won lessons and prevent young entrepreneurs from repeating mistakes.

- **Intellectual Stimulation:** Stay engaged with the business world and be exposed to fresh ideas.

- **Vicarious Entrepreneurship:** Experience the thrill of innovation with less personal risk involved.

- **Give Back to the Business Community:** Foster a strong entrepreneurial ecosystem that benefits everyone.

Getting Started:

- **Mentorship Programs:** Local universities, business incubators, or organizations like SCORE connect mentors with startups.

- **Define Your Niche:** Do you gravitate towards tech, social enterprise, or a specific industry you know well?

- **Openness to Diverse Styles:** Embrace different approaches to business, offering guidance without imposing your 'way'.

Resources Needed:

- **Local Startup Scene:** Identify accelerators, business schools, or co-working spaces with a focus on early-stage ventures.

- **Mentorship Models:** Familiarize yourself with different mentorship formats (one-on-one, group, short-term, etc.).

- **Online Networks:** Platforms dedicated to startup mentorship can expand your reach and options.

Challenges and Tips:

- **Startup Tempo:** Be prepared for a fast-paced, iterative environment where mistakes are part of learning.

- **Communication is Key:** Emphasize clear feedback that balances honesty with encouragement.

- **It's Their Journey:** Guide them in decision-making without imposing your own vision for their company.

Ways to Deepen the Experience:

- **Specialized Expertise:** Offer talks on legal matters, fundraising, or areas relevant to your skills.

- **Long-Term Relationships:** Become a trusted advisor over time, supporting milestones and challenges.

- **Peer Mentor Community:** Connect with other retired professionals and pool your collective wisdom.

Safety and Accessibility:

- **Time Commitment Clarified:** Set clear expectations for the frequency and duration of your mentorship.

- **Formal vs Informal:** Structured programs provide more defined roles while informal arrangements offer flexibility.

- **Mutual Respect:** Emphasize a collaborative dynamic, valuing the entrepreneur's drive and vision.

Call to Action:

Ready to share your entrepreneurial expertise and shape the next generation of business leaders? Seek out Startup Mentorship opportunities near you!

Animal Welfare Advocate

Champion for Furry Friends: Become an Animal Welfare Advocate

Brief Description:

DEDICATE YOUR TIME, ENERGY, and voice to improving the lives of animals. From hands-on volunteering at local shelters to organizing initiatives supporting animal welfare, you can play a vital role in promoting responsible pet ownership, adoption, and reducing animal suffering.

Why It's Great for Retirees:

- **Combine Passion and Purpose:** Turn your love for animals into tangible action and advocacy.

- **Diverse Volunteer Needs:** Tasks for all abilities – walking dogs, fostering, fundraising, and more.

- **Sense of Community:** Connect with like-minded animal lovers, fostering friendships and mutual support.

- **Emotional Rewards:** The love and gratitude received from animals bring immeasurable joy.

Getting Started

- **Shelters and Rescue Organizations:** Inquire about volunteer needs and orientations.

- **Advocacy Initiatives:** Identify current local issues (spay/neuter campaigns, legislation, etc.).

- **Utilize Your Skills:** Bring your talents to the cause – photography, writing, event organizing, and more.

Resources Needed

- **Local Animal Welfare Landscape:** Shelters, rescue groups, organizations focusing on specific animal needs.

- **Online Resources:** Best Friends Animal Society, ASPCA, etc., offer information and advocacy toolkits.

- **Social Networks:** Connect with other regional animal welfare advocates for collaboration and support.

Challenges and Tips

- **Emotional Toll:** Be prepared for the reality of animal suffering. Practice self-care and lean on the community.

- **Persistence is Key:** Advocacy can be slow – celebrate small wins alongside long-term goals.

- **People Skills Too:** Volunteers interact with the public, and advocacy may involve navigating opinions.

Ways to Deepen the Experience:

- **Foster and Adoption Focus:** Provide vital temporary homes and help animals find forever families.

- **Target a Specific Animal:** Support breed-specific rescues or specialize in senior pets or animals with special needs.

- **Policy Change Advocacy:** Get involved with efforts to strengthen animal protection laws at the local level.

Safety and Accessibility:

- **Realistic Expectations:** Match your volunteer role to your physical capabilities and emotional bandwidth.

- **Respectful Animal Interactions:** Shelters often offer training for volunteers on proper animal handling.

- **Team Support:** Advocacy is most effective as a collective effort, ensuring ongoing support for volunteers.

Call to Action:

Ready to stand up for those who cannot speak for themselves? Connect with your local Animal Welfare organizations and find your way to make a difference!

40

Food Security Initiatives

Fight Hunger, Build Community: Join Food Security Initiatives

Brief Description:

FOOD INSECURITY AFFECTS PEOPLE of all ages, right in your own neighborhood. Combat this issue by volunteering at food pantries, starting community gardens, teaching cooking basics, or advocating for policies that ensure everyone has access to healthy and affordable food.

Why It's Great for Retirees:

- **Make a Direct Impact:** See your efforts immediately benefit those in need.

- **Diverse Ways to Help:** Opportunities for all skill levels, from physical work to advocacy.

- **Bridging Generations:** Teach kids about gardening, help struggling families learn to budget and cook.

- **Community Connection:** Collaborate with neighbors across ages and backgrounds for a shared sense of purpose.

Getting Started:

- **Existing Organizations:** Food banks, soup kitchens, and community gardens often rely on volunteers.

- **Identify Gaps:** Are there specific needs (senior food insecurity, cooking education) you could address?

- **Your Passion Points:** Do you love to garden, cook, organize? Lean into your strengths to be most effective.

Resources Needed:

- **Local Anti-Hunger Landscape:** Map out organizations focusing on specific aspects of food security.

- **Funding and Partnerships:** Explore potential grants or partnerships with grocery stores or restaurants.

- **Volunteer Community:** Success often relies on consistent helpers, so fostering a team is key.

Challenges and Tips:

- **Root Causes Matter:** Addressing hunger goes beyond handouts, so understand the wider issues at play.

- **Sustainability is Key:** Short-term fixes are good, but long-term solutions (gardens, policy change) are crucial.

- **Collaboration, Not Competition:** Work with existing efforts rather than duplicating and straining resources.

Ways to Deepen the Experience:

- **Focus on Healthy Food:** Advocate for access to fresh produce and nutrition education.

- **Intergenerational Meal Programs:** Bridge gaps and provide social connection by pairing seniors and kids.

- **Waste Not, Want Not:** Partner with businesses to collect 'ugly' produce or near-expiration food for donation.

Safety and Accessibility:

- **Varied Roles for All Abilities:** Offer a range of tasks, ensuring everyone can participate and feel valued.

- **Food Safety Training:** If handling food, ensure volunteers understand proper practices.

- **Respectful Service:** When serving those experiencing insecurity, prioritize dignity and kindness.

Call to Action:

Ready to roll up your sleeves and fight for a world where no one goes hungry? Discover Food Security Initiatives in your community and start making a difference!

41

Global Education Volunteers

Empower Young Minds: Become a Global Education Volunteer

Brief Description:

EXPAND YOUR HORIZONS AND make a lasting contribution to communities around the world. Volunteer in educational projects, working alongside local teachers to build schools, teach English or other vital skills, empower girls through education, or support special needs learners in underprivileged communities.

Why It's Great for Retirees:

- **Share Your Knowledge:** Your skills and life experience are invaluable assets for others.

- **Immersive Cultural Experience:** Go beyond tourism and truly connect with different cultures

- **Adventure with Purpose:** Blend travel with the satisfaction of making a tangible difference.

- **New Perspective:** Challenge your worldview and gain a deeper appreciation for global interconnectedness.

Getting Started:

- **Reputable Programs:** Research organizations with strong track records, safety protocols, and local partnerships. (Habitat for Humanity Global Village, Cross-Cultural Solutions, etc.).

- **Honest Self-Assessment:** Consider your health, adaptability, and language skills for the best fit.

- **Commitment Level:** Programs range from short-term to multi-week immersions with varying intensity.

Resources Needed:

- **Volunteer Matching Websites:** Idealist, Globalteer, and others often list educational volunteer projects.

- **Program-Specific Information:** Each organization provides details on locations, skills needed, trip costs, etc.

- **Local Connections:** Seek out others who have done similar programs for firsthand experiences and tips.

Challenges and Tips:

- **Language Barriers:** Some basic phrases in the local language are helpful, but patience is key.

- **"Helping" vs. "Imposing":** Local partners will guide you on culturally sensitive, sustainable aid.

- **Emotional Impact:** Witnessing poverty or educational disparities can be difficult; prioritize self-care.

Ways to Deepen the Experience:

- **Skill-Specific Programs:** If you're a retired teacher, doctor, etc., find programs that leverage your expertise.

- **Host Family Option:** Living with a local family offers unparalleled cultural immersion and bonds.

- **Combine Passions:** If you love hiking, seek projects in scenic regions! This adds to your enjoyment.

Safety and Accessibility:

- **Thorough Trip Briefing:** Organizations should cover health precautions, emergency plans, etc.

- **Choose Wisely:** Some projects involve more physical labor than others, matching your abilities is crucial.

- **Insurance and Support:** Ensure the program offers adequate coverage and in-country assistance if needed.

Call to Action:

Ready to use your skills to empower young minds and broaden your own horizons? Explore Global Education Volunteer opportunities and unlock a world of purpose-driven adventure!

42

Aquaponics Systems

Become a Backyard Farmer and Fishkeeper: Create Your Own Aquaponics System

Brief Description:

AQUAPONICS IS A CLOSED-LOOP system where fish and plants benefit each other. Fish waste fertilizes plants grown hydroponically, and the plants clean water for the fish. This setup allows you to produce fresh, organic vegetables and fish right in your own home or backyard.

Why It's Great for Retirees:

- **Sustainable Food Source:** Enjoy home-grown produce and potentially raise your own fish for consumption.

- **Geeky Fun Factor:** Aquaponics blends biology, engineering, and gardening, making it intellectually stimulating.

- **Scalable to Your Space:** Systems can be small countertop setups or large backyard operations.

- **Rewarding Learning Curve:** Enjoy the process of optimizing and nurturing a complex mini-ecosystem.

Getting Started:

- **Size and Setup:** Determine if you want an indoor/outdoor, DIY/pre-built system.

- **The Knowledge Base:** Research is key! Learn about fish species, suitable plants, and system maintenance.

- **Community is Key:** Online forums and local groups offer invaluable advice and potential resources.

Resources Needed:

- **Aquaponics Resources:** Websites, books, and YouTube channels explain the science and practical setup.

- **Building Supplies or Systems:** Depending on your path, from basic tanks to pre-fabricated units.

- **Grow Lights (Indoors):** If natural light is limited, invest in suitable grow lights for your plants.

Challenges and Tips:

- **Start Small, Expand Later:** Avoid being overwhelmed; success breeds confidence to scale up.

- **Balancing Act:** Mastering nutrient levels and water quality is key but comes with trial and error.

- **Not Maintenance-Free:** Regular monitoring and upkeep are essential for a healthy system.

Ways to Deepen the Experience:

- **Edible + Ornamental:** Blend herbs, salad greens, and even flowering plants for aesthetics.

- **Focus on Fish:** Raise edible fish like tilapia or ornamental varieties like koi depending on your goal.

- **"Upcycle" Existing Gear:** Repurposing an old aquarium or containers can make it budget-friendly.

Safety and Accessibility:

- **Food-Safe Materials:** Ensure all components won't leach harmful chemicals into your food.

- **Electrical Safety (Indoors):** Secure wiring, especially around water, to prevent any hazards.

- **System Weight:** Large setups need stable bases, consider this alongside accessibility for maintenance.

Call to Action:

Ready to dive into a rewarding and sustainable hobby? Start exploring the world of aquaponics and discover the joy of a homegrown closed-loop ecosystem!

Home and Garden

43

Eco-Friendly Home Makeovers

Go Green at Home: Workshops on Sustainable Home Makeovers

Brief Description:

GET EMPOWERED TO MAKE your home more eco-conscious! Learn practical strategies to improve energy efficiency, switch to sustainable materials, reduce waste, and create a healthier living environment. Workshops go beyond theory to provide hands-on guidance and resources for impactful change.

Why It's Great for Retirees:

- **Direct Impact on Your Space:** Make tangible improvements with long-term benefits for you and the planet.

- **Cost-Saving Potential:** Energy efficiency upgrades and waste reduction can lower your bills over time.

- **Step-by-Step is Key:** Makes eco-living less overwhelming by breaking down large projects.

- **Learn and Do!:** Provides both knowledge and the motivation to finally tackle those home projects.

Getting Started:

- **Tap into Local Expertise:** Seek workshops by utility companies, sustainable home stores, or community groups.

- **Your Focus Area:** Choose general overviews or workshops specific to water saving, solar energy, etc.

- **Hands-On Element:** The best workshops let you try things, from testing insulation to seeing efficient appliances.

Resources Needed:

- **Workshop Listings:** Check libraries, community centers, even some hardware stores may offer these.

- **Online Resources:** Search for [Your Area] Sustainable Home Workshops to find potential providers.

- **Incentive Programs:** Research local or state rebates for energy upgrades your workshop may highlight.

Challenges and Tips:

- **Realistic Expectations:** Home makeovers take time and investment, workshops are a starting point.

- **Prioritize the High-Impact:** Focus on changes with the biggest environmental (and cost-saving) benefit first.

- **DIY vs Hiring Out:** Workshops can help you decide what you can tackle yourself and when to call a pro.

Ways to Deepen the Experience:

- **"Show and Tell" Tours:** Can some workshops include a visit to a model eco-friendly home?

- **Product Demos:** Comparing low-flow showerheads, eco-friendly paints, etc. is highly informative.

- **Long-Term Support:** Ideal programs connect you to resources (contractors, rebates) beyond the workshop.

Safety and Accessibility:

- **Ability Inclusive:** Some workshops may offer demos with adaptive tools or focus on simple retrofits.

- **Home Assessments:** Are in-home energy audits offered on their own or as a follow-up service?

- **Trusted Providers:** Ensure those leading workshops are experts, not pushing specific products for profit.

Call to Action:

Ready to turn your house into an eco-haven? Search for Eco-Friendly Home Makeover workshops in your area and take the first step towards a healthier home and healthier planet!

44

Heritage Seed Collecting

Become a Seed Saver: Discover the Wonders of Heritage Seeds

Brief Description:

Turn gardening into an act of preservation! Collect and cultivate heirloom seeds - plant varieties passed down for generations with unique flavors and rich histories. Contribute to biodiversity, become a part of plant history, and enjoy the fruits (and veggies) of your labor!

Why It's Great for Retirees:

- **Connecting with History:** Each seed holds a story, unearthing fascinating tales of human and plant migration.

- **Rewarding Challenge:** Learning seed saving techniques adds a new layer of skill to your gardening practice.

- **Community of Seed Savers:** Tap into a passionate network of enthusiasts eager to share and trade seeds.

- **A Legacy Project:** Passing on collected seeds to future generations leaves a beautiful, living mark.

Getting Started:

- **Learn the Basics:** Seed saving requires specific practices, so books, websites, or workshops are essential.

- **Start with "Easy" Seeds:** Beans, tomatoes, some flowers are more beginner-friendly than others.

- **Seed Sources:** Farmer's markets, local seed swaps, and reputable online sellers (Seed Savers Exchange, etc.).

Resources Needed:

- **Seed Saving Resources:** Look for beginner-friendly guides and local organizations focused on heritage seeds.

- **Seed Storage Supplies:** Small envelopes, glass jars, and proper labeling are vital for organization.

- **Community is Key:** Seed swaps, gardening groups, and online forums are rich sources of knowledge and support.

Challenges and Tips:

- **Not All Seeds Are Equal:** Some plants cross-pollinate easily, requiring more complex saving methods.

- **The Legalities Matter:** While most saving is fine, be aware of patented seeds and restrictions.

- **Sharing is Caring:** The point is to spread these seeds, don't just hoard your collection!

Ways to Deepen the Experience:

- **Focus on Your Region:** Seek out heritage seeds adapted to your climate for thriving plants.

- **Seed Stories:** Record the history of your seeds and share them with others as you pass them on.

- **Organize a Seed Swap:** Turn your hobby into a community-building event for fellow gardeners.

Safety and Accessibility:

- **Physical Demands:** While mostly low-impact, seed saving does involve some fine motor skills.

- **Plant Allergies:** Factor in any sensitivities when choosing what seeds to collect.

- **Open Door Policy:** Seed swaps are a fantastic way to find the seeds you want and welcome new gardeners.

Call to Action:

Ready to become a custodian of plant history? Start exploring the world of heritage seeds and add a unique dimension to your gardening!

45

Smart Kitchen Hacks

Upgrade Your Kitchen Tech: Discover Smart Kitchen Hacks

Brief Description:

GET TECH-SAVVY IN THE kitchen! Explore how smart ovens, appliances, and apps can streamline meal planning, make cooking more efficient, reduce food waste, and even help you become a better cook.

Why It's Great for Retirees:

- **Simplify Cooking Tasks:** Voice-controlled appliances, recipe apps... tech can lessen the load for hands-on prep.

- **Minimize Waste, Save Money:** Apps help utilize leftovers, find deals, and manage expiry dates.

- **New Culinary Adventures:** Tech can spark trying new recipes, with less fear of failure due to guided support.

- **Fun Factor:** Play with gadgets while feeling current with the latest tech trends.

Getting Started:

- **Target Pain Points:** Do you hate meal planning? Overbuy groceries? Start with solving one problem.

- **Ease of Use is Key:** Avoid overly complicated devices, focus on user-friendly smart tech.

- **Small Steps, Big Gains:** Maybe it's just a smart speaker for recipe lookups to begin with.

Resources Needed:

- **Gadget Reviews:** Which smart products actually deliver on promises? Seek trustworthy sources.

- **Recipe Apps & Platforms:** Some are free, others subscription-based, explore options.

- **Community and Support:** Tech support from the store or online forums can be vital for troubleshooting.

Challenges and Tips:

- **Cost vs. Benefit:** Is a fancy smart fridge worth it? Weigh this carefully against your needs.

- **The Novelty Factor:** Don't let the shiny gadgetry replace cooking basics - it's a tool, not a chef.

- **Not Infallible:** Smart recipes still need taste-testing, and tech can malfunction!

Ways to Deepen the Experience:

- **Focus on Specific Needs:** Dietary restrictions or allergies? There are apps for that!

- **Virtual Cooking Classes:** Some platforms pair with smart appliances for guided learning.

- **Sharing Good Finds:** Become the "tech scout" for your friends, sharing tips and successful hacks.

Safety and Accessibility:

- **Security and Updates:** Be aware of any data privacy concerns with certain devices.

- **Accessible Tech:** Look for voice-controlled options or those with large displays for ease of use.

- **Not a Replacement:** Smart kitchens can help, but don't assume they'll do everything for you.

Call to Action:

Ready to give your kitchen a tech makeover? Start exploring the world of Smart Kitchen Hacks and see how they can make mealtimes easier and more fun!

46

Tiny House Building

Downsizing Dreams: Explore the World of Tiny House Building

Brief Description:

GET HANDS-ON WITH THE tiny house movement! Design or even embark on the adventure of building your own tiny home – a space that prioritizes intentional living, sustainability, and maximizing efficiency over sheer square footage.

Why It's Great for Retirees:

- **Lower Cost of Living:** Tiny homes can be more affordable to build, own, and maintain long-term.expand_more

- **Freedom and Flexibility:** Potential for easier relocation, a lock-and-leave lifestyle, or space for aging in place.

- **Hands-On Challenge:** A project for retirees who enjoy DIY, problem-solving, and learning new skills.

- **Sustainability Focus:** Forces mindful consumption and aligns with eco-conscious values.exclamation

Getting Started:

- **Your "Why"?** Is this full-time living, a guest house, an income property? Purpose guides design.

- **Be Realistic About Skills:** DIY requires building know-how, or you'll need a contractor.

- **Zoning Laws MATTER:** Where you park it is crucial. Don't build without knowing if it's legal.

Resources Needed:

- **Builder Community:** Tiny house workshops, online forums, and experts are vital for knowledge sharing.

- **Design Plans and Resources:** Explore pre-made tiny house plans or customize your own.

- **Local Regulations:** Understand zoning restrictions, building codes, and potential permits needed.

Challenges and Tips:

- **The Build is TOUGH:** Physically demanding, even with kits.exclamation Be honest about your capabilities.

- **Living Tiny Isn't Easy:** Close quarters, minimalism... it's a major lifestyle adjustment, not just cute decor.

- **"Parking" is Paramount:** Finding a legal, hookup-equipped spot for your tiny home is often the BIGGEST hurdle.

Ways to Deepen the Experience:

- **Focus on Off-Grid:** Incorporate solar, composting toilets, etc., for truly self-sufficient living.

- **Skill Share:** Workshops on tiny home wiring, plumbing, etc., are empowering (even if you later hire out).

- **Community Living:** Explore tiny house co-ops or communities for mutual support and shared resources.

Safety and Accessibility:

- **Codes and Inspections:** Even DIY may need professional input to ensure safety standards are met.

- **Aging in Place Design:** Consider accessibility needs from the start for possible future limitations.

- **Legal and Secure:** Proper permitting and insurance are vital, especially for full-time tiny home living.

Call to Action:

Intrigued by downsizing and the DIY challenge? Dive into the world of Tiny House Building and see if it sparks a new chapter!

47

Backyard Beekeeping

Backyard Buzz: Become a Beekeeper

Brief Description:

DISCOVER THE FASCINATING WORLD of bees and create a haven for pollinators in your own backyard. With proper training and equipment, you can manage beehives, harvest delicious honey, and contribute to the health of your local ecosystem.

Why It's Great for Retirees:

- **Meaningful and Rewarding:** Play an active role in supporting bee populations and learn about their importance.

- **Gentle Physical Activity:** Hive tending involves lifting and movement, but at a manageable pace.

- **Mental Stimulation:** Beekeeping keeps you learning, from hive dynamics to understanding seasons and blooms.

- **Foodie Factor:** The honey is a delicious bonus, and might inspire new culinary adventures.

Getting Started:

- **Beekeeping Legality:** Check local regulations, some areas have ordinances, others none at all.

- **Join a Beekeeping Association:** The BEST starting point for training, mentorship, and community.

- **Start Slow:** Begin with one or two hives and focus on mastering the basics before expanding.

Resources Needed:

- **Local Beekeeping Resources:** Seek out classes, bee supply stores, and experienced mentors.

- **Protective Gear:** Essential for safety while working with the bees (suit, smoker, gloves, etc.).

- **Hive Setup:** Hives, frames, necessary tools, and a suitable location in your backyard.

Challenges and Tips:

- **Commitment Matters:** Bees need year-round care, not just a summer hobby. Be prepared for the cycle.

- **Not for the Highly Allergic:** Stings are a reality, ensure it's safe based on your health.

- **Neighbor Education:** Proactively address potential concerns, showcasing the ecological benefits.

Ways to Deepen the Experience:

- **Native Pollinator Plants:** Landscape with plants attracting not just honeybees, but other vital pollinators.

- **Wax Wonders:** Learn about beeswax uses: candles, salves, etc., for additional crafty projects.

- **Sharing the Knowledge:** Offer hive tours for kids or host beginner beekeeping talks to inspire others.

Safety and Accessibility:

- **Proper Training is Key:** Emphasize safe handling practices to minimize stings.

- **Allergy Awareness:** Have an epi-pen on hand (even if not previously allergic, reactions can worsen).

- **Mindful Placement:** Situate hives away from high-traffic areas to avoid accidental encounters.

Call to Action:

Ready to welcome a gentle buzz into your backyard? Connect with your local beekeeping community and begin your journey of supporting pollinators and reaping the sweet rewards!

48

Home Brewery and Winery

Cheers to Crafting Your Own: Explore Home Brewing and Winemaking

Brief Description:

BECOME A MASTER OF fermentation! Dive into the craft of making your own beer or wine in the comfort of your home. Learn the science behind the process, experiment with flavors, and perhaps create a signature vintage to share with loved ones.

Why It's Great for Retirees:

- **Creative Expression:** Craft beverages allow endless experimentation to personalize your creations.

- **Satisfying Process:** From ingredient selection to bottling, seeing (and tasting!) your finished product is rewarding.

- **Social Element:** Sharing your creations, learning with fellow enthusiasts fosters a sense of community.

- **Pride in the Pour:** Nothing quite like serving guests a beverage you crafted yourself.

Getting Started:

- **Beer or Wine?** Choose based on your interest, but be aware they require slightly different equipment.

- **Start Simple:** Kits are a great intro, letting you grasp the basics before going all-grain or fancy grapes.

- **Knowledge is Key:** Brewing/winemaking books, online guides, or local classes are essential.

Resources Needed:

- **Brewing/Winemaking Resources:** Local supply shops, online guides, and fellow hobbyists are invaluable.

- **Space and Equipment:** Depending on the scale, it could be a countertop setup or a dedicated "brew room".

- **Quality Ingredients:** Kits simplify this, but eventually you'll be sourcing your own for unique creations.

Challenges and Tips:

- **Cleanliness is Key:** Sanitation is vital to avoid spoiling your batch – the fun stuff takes meticulous prep.

- **It's a Science:** Fermentation isn't just waiting, so be prepared for some chemistry and trial and error.

- **Patience Pays Off:** Especially with wine, aging is part of the process... delayed gratification!

Ways to Deepen the Experience:

- **Grow Your Own Ingredients:** Hops or grapes (depending on climate) add a whole new level to the craft.

- **Specialty Styles:** Explore sours, barrel-aged beers, fortified wines... there's always more to learn.

- **"Tasting and Tweaking" Sessions:** Invite friends for feedback to refine your recipes.

Safety and Accessibility:

- **Responsible Consumption:** Moderation matters, especially when the supply is self-produced!

- **Food Safety First:** Proper techniques prevent contamination that could ruin an entire batch.

- **Mind the Mess:** Especially with bottling, set up a workspace that can handle potential spills.

Call to Action:

Ready to unleash your inner vintner or brewmaster? Explore the world of Home Brewing and Winemaking – a delicious adventure awaits!

49

Rainwater Harvesting Systems

Catch the Rain: Explore Rainwater Harvesting Systems for Your Home

Why It's Great for Retirees:

- **Save Money:** Reduce reliance on municipal water, potentially lowering your water bills.

- **Good for the Environment:** Conserve a precious resource and lessen your home's environmental impact.

- **Promote Plant Growth:** Rainwater is naturally soft and free of chemicals, ideal for nurturing gardens.

- **Sense of Accomplishment:** Seeing a system you set up collect and provide water can be very rewarding.

Types of Rainwater Harvesting Systems:

- **Rain Barrel System:** A simple and affordable option that collects rainwater from your roof downspout.

- **Cisterns:** Larger underground tanks that store greater quantities of rainwater.

- **Whole-House Systems:** More complex systems that can provide rainwater for most household uses (excluding toilets and drinking water).

Getting Started:

- **Local Regulations:** Check local ordinances to ensure rainwater harvesting is permitted in your area.

- **Rainwater Uses:** Identify how you'll use the collected water (watering plants, washing cars, etc.).

- **Roof Size and Rainfall:** The size of your system depends on the amount of rainwater you can collect.

Resources Needed:

- **Rainwater Harvesting Supplies:** Barrels, pumps, filters (depending on your chosen system).

- **Installation Help:** Consider hiring a professional for complex systems or if you're not comfortable with DIY projects.

- **Gardening Resources:** Learn about rainwater usage for optimal plant growth.

Challenges and Tips:

- **Initial Investment:** The cost of equipment and installation varies, but factor in long-term water bill savings.

- **Maintenance:** Regular cleaning and filter changes are necessary to keep your system functioning properly.

- **Winter Considerations:** In cold climates, you may need to winterize your system to prevent freezing.

Ways to Deepen the Experience:

- **Expand Your System:** Start with a rain barrel and gradually add more storage capacity as needed.

- **Connect to Your Garden:** Set up an irrigation system for automated watering from your rainwater storage.

- **Share Your Knowledge:** Encourage friends and neighbors to explore rainwater harvesting.

Safety and Accessibility:

- **Mosquito Control:** Properly fitted screens prevent mosquitos from breeding in your rainwater storage.

- **Drinking Water Treatment:** Rainwater is not generally suitable for drinking without proper filtration and disinfection.

- **Physical Considerations:** Lifting heavy buckets of water may require adjustments for those with limitations.

Call to Action:

READY TO DO YOUR part for the environment and potentially save money? Explore Rainwater Harvesting Systems and start collecting that rainwater!

50

Solar Power Projects

Harness the Sun: Explore DIY Solar Power Projects

Brief Description:

GET HANDS-ON WITH SOLAR power! Learn how to incorporate solar energy into your home – from simple DIY projects like solar-powered lights to potentially larger installations like rooftop panels. Reduce your energy costs, lessen environmental impact, and gain the satisfaction of producing some of your own power.

Why It's Great for Retirees:

- **Fight Rising Energy Costs:** Solar offsets consumption, potentially lowering your bills over time.

- **Environmental Stewardship:** Contribute to a sustainable energy future, leaving a lighter footprint.

- **Scalable to Your Comfort:** Start small or embrace the challenge of bigger solar projects.

- **Educational and Rewarding:** Learn about solar technology and feel accomplished when it works!

Getting Started:

- **Local Regulations and Incentives:** Check what's allowed, and any rebates that reduce installation costs.

- **Honest Skill Assessment:** Some DIY is safe, others are truly for electricians - know your limits.

- **Start Simple (and Safe):** Solar path lights, charging stations, etc., build confidence before major projects.

Resources Needed:

- **Solar 101:** Understand the basics: panel types, inverters... online resources or even library books.

- **Project-Specific Knowledge:** Seek out detailed guides and communities if doing complex installations.

- **Tools and Safety Gear:** Beyond standard DIY, solar may require specific electrical tools and safety focus.

Challenges and Tips:

- **Initial Cost vs. Long-Term:** Solar can be an investment upfront, but factor in potential savings.

- **DIY vs. Professional:** Don't endanger yourself. Complex panel installations often require electricians.

- **Sun is Not Constant:** Understand your region's solar potential and any need for battery backup.

Ways to Deepen the Experience:

- **Going Off-Grid (Partially):** Can you power your shed entirely on solar? Challenges you to get efficient.

- **Solar Gadgets:** Build solar-powered phone chargers, fountain pumps, etc., for techy fun.

- **Teaching Others:** Host a "solar party" showcasing your smaller projects to inspire neighbors.

Safety and Accessibility:

- **Electrical Safety PARAMOUNT:** Solar is still electricity, respect the risks, especially with DIY.

- **Roof Work Considerations:** Panel installation may not be advisable if heights are a concern.

- **Accessibility of Information:** Ensure the guides you use are clear and match your skill level.

Call to Action:

Ready to power your home with sunshine? Explore DIY Solar Projects and unlock the potential of renewable energy!

51

Vertical Forest Walls

Build a Breathing Wall: Create a Vertical Forest Inside or Outside Your Home

Brief Description:

TRANSFORM A PLAIN WALL into a living tapestry of plants! Vertical gardening offers a space-saving, visually stunning way to boost indoor air quality, add greenery to limited outdoor spaces, or even grow your own herbs and veggies in a vertical format.

Why It's Great for Retirees:

- **Low-Maintenance Beauty:** Many vertical systems have built-in irrigation, taking the guesswork out of watering.

- **Mental and Physical Benefits:** Tending plants is calming, and a vertical wall adds a dose of nature indoors.

- **Scalable to Your Space:** From big statement walls to countertop herb gardens, it can fit any home.

- **Creative Expression:** Endless opportunities to design with different plants, colors, and textures.

Getting Started:

- **Wall or Freestanding:** DIY frames, pre-made pocket systems, all have pros and cons to consider.

- **Indoors vs. Outdoors:** Light source is KEY. Indoors may need grow lights, outdoors factor in sun angle.

- **Plant Possibilities:** Leafy greens, air-purifying plants, colorful succulents - tailor to your goals.

Resources Needed:

- **Construction Know-How:** DIY requires basic skills, or there are ready-to-plant commercial systems.

- **Vertical Gardening Guides:** Specific to the system you choose, as proper setup is crucial.

- **Plant Sourcing:** Beyond the typical nursery, seek out interesting textures or even edible options.

Challenges and Tips:

- **Weight and Water:** Ensure your wall can handle it, especially with saturated soil (indoors is key).

- **Not Maintenance-Free:** Systems streamline it, but you'll still prune, refill reservoirs, etc.

- **The Right Fit:** Some plants are easier in vertical systems than others - research is your friend.

Ways to Deepen the Experience:

- **Air Purifying Powerhouse:** Research the best plants for this, creating a functional AND beautiful wall.

- **Vertical Herb Garden:** Fresh flavors at your fingertips, replacing spice jars with a living pantry.

- **"Evolving Artwork":** Choose plants with changing foliage, making the wall a dynamic piece over seasons.

Safety and Accessibility:

- **Weight Considerations:** Can you safely lift/hang/maintain, or do you need a lighter system?

- **Food Safety:** If growing edibles, ensure fertilizers are safe, and proper harvesting methods are used.

- **Leak Prevention:** Indoors especially, ensure excess water is contained and won't damage your walls.

Call to Action:

Ready to bring a touch of the wild into your home? Explore Vertical Forest Walls and transform your space!

52

Genealogical Journeys

Genealogical Journeys: Chart the Living Branches of Your Family Tree

Brief Description:

EMBARK ON A TRAVEL experience that transforms your ancestry from names and dates into vivid places and personal stories. Visit ancestral towns, explore historical archives, and connect with your family's past in a way no website or document could ever replicate.

Why It's Great for Retirees:

- **Legacy Building:** Deepen your understanding of your family's journey, leaving a more detailed and tangible legacy for generations to come.

- **Sense of Purpose:** Retirement offers the perfect time for an immersive and meaningful project like a genealogical journey.

- **Travel with Meaning:** Infuse your travels with added significance and connection.

- **Unexpected Discoveries:** Unearth hidden family stories, distant relatives, and new branches on your family tree.

Getting Started:

- **Focus Your Journey:** Choose a specific lineage, time period, or geographical area to guide your journey.

- **Partner with a Specialist:** Genealogists specializing in travel can help plan research, destinations, and logistics.

- **Map Your Route:** Pinpoint towns, villages, record repositories – not just tourist destinations.

Resources Needed:

- **Family Tree Foundation:** Begin with existing records, DNA results, etc., to provide clues for your journey.

- **Archival Access:** Contact repositories in targeted locations in advance to ensure access to records.

- **Language Skills:** Basic language skills for your destination can be helpful (or consider a translator/guide).

Challenges and Tips:

- **Unexpected Roadblocks:** Records may be incomplete or damaged, locations may have changed – patience is key!

- **Emotional Impact:** Prepare for deeply personal moments, both joyful and potentially difficult.

- **Beyond Tourism:** Be prepared for less 'glamorous' aspects of travel focused on historical research and rural areas.

Ways to Deepen the Experience:

- **Thematic Journeys:** Center your journey around your ancestors' occupation, historical events, or migrations.

- **Cultural Immersion:** Learn about local traditions and cuisine to understand ancestors' daily lives.

- **Meet Local Historians:** Local archives or societies may have deeper knowledge of your family's place in the area.

Safety and Accessibility:

- **Travel Fitness:** Ensure the level of walking, transportation, etc. is comfortable for your abilities.

- **Research Reputability:** Work with established genealogists and companies for a safe, productive journey.

- **Secure Documentation:** Always have backups of important family documents and research while traveling.

Call to Action:

Are you ready to transform your understanding of your family history? Explore Genealogical Journeys and step back in time!

Travel and Adventure

53

Houseboat Living Experiences

Title: Houseboat Living Experience: Embrace Waterways and a Simpler Life

Brief Description:

IMMERSE YOURSELF IN THE unique rhythm of life afloat. Swap land-locked living for a month-long houseboat adventure – learn the ropes of boat handling, explore picturesque waterways, and embrace the tranquility of water-based living.

Why It's Great for Retirees:

- **New Adventures:** Retirement is the perfect time to branch out and try something completely different.

- **Slower Pace:** Escape the hustle and bustle for a more relaxed pace of life.

- **Scenic Exploration:** Gently discover hidden waterways, charming towns, and unique wildlife encounters from your floating home.

- **Sense of Community:** The houseboat community is known for its camaraderie and shared experiences.

Getting Started:

- **Rental vs. Purchase:** For a trial experience, rental is the ideal way to see if it suits your lifestyle.

- **Location, Location:** Choose a network of waterways that offers the balance of scenery and amenities you prefer.

- **Boat Size and Type:** Consider how much space you'll need and the style of houseboat (narrowboat, cruiser, etc.).

Resources Needed:

- **Boating Basics:** Take a short course or hire instruction if you're new to boat handling and navigation.

- **Waterway Guides:** Charts, maps, and local knowledge help you plan routes and understand locks, moorings, etc.

- **Houseboat Specifics:** Learn the systems of your chosen boat (power, waste disposal, etc.).

Challenges and Tips:

- **Embrace the Learning Curve:** Operating a boat takes skill, be patient with yourself.

- **Limited Space:** Minimalism is your friend on a houseboat, pack mindfully.

- **Shared Waterways:** Be considerate of other boaters and follow waterway rules.

Ways to Deepen the Experience:

- **Embrace Self-Sufficiency:** Learn about solar power, water systems, and off-grid living if applicable.

- **Go Fishing:** Try your hand at catching dinner from your front porch.

- **Nature Connection:** Birdwatching, stargazing, and simply enjoying the views take center stage.

Safety and Accessibility:

- **Life Jackets:** Non-negotiable for everyone onboard.

- **Mobility Considerations:** Choose a boat layout that's easy to navigate.

- **Emergency Plan:** Know how to signal for help and have a plan in case of mechanical issues.

Call to Action:

Is a month-long houseboat adventure calling your name? Explore rental options and cast off into a new and fulfilling chapter of your life!

54

Photography Tours with a Twist

Photography Tours with a Twist: Capture Stories, Not Just Sights

Brief Description:

DIVE DEEPER THAN POSTCARD-PERFECT landscapes on photography tours that combine technical skill with immersive cultural experiences. Document festivals, daily rituals, artisans at work – capture the essence of a place through its people and traditions.

Why It's Great for Retirees:

- **Purposeful Travel:** Turn your photography passion into a force for connection and understanding.

- **Creative Growth:** Push beyond scenic shots, honing your skills to tell impactful visual stories.

- **Authentic Encounters:** Build rapport with locals as you respectfully photograph their lives and traditions.

- **Enduring Memories:** Create a portfolio with depth, bringing home more than just pretty pictures.

Getting Started:

- **Choose Your Focus:** Festivals, specific crafts, daily life – what sparks your curiosity?

- **Find the Right Tour:** Companies specialize in this niche, emphasizing respect and ethical photography.

- **Brush Up on Skills:** Portraiture, street photography, and understanding light are all key.

Resources Needed:

- **Flexible Camera Gear:** Landscapes are still part of it, so versatility is important (lens choices, etc.).

- **Cultural Sensitivity Guide:** Your tour provider should offer this – do's, don'ts, how to interact.

- **People Skills:** Smiles and gestures go a long way, even with limited language skills.

Challenges and Tips:

- **Going Beyond the Obvious:** Seek out the less-photographed moments that tell the truer story.

- **Respect is Paramount:** Ask permission, understand boundaries, and ensure your presence isn't intrusive.

- **Letting Go of Control:** Street photography is unpredictable – embrace the spontaneity.

Ways to Deepen the Experience:

- **Learn the Language:** A few basic phrases open doors and ease interactions.

- **Give Back:** Offer prints to those you photograph, or find ways to support local initiatives.

- **Blog or Exhibit:** Turn your trip into a curated story to share with others and raise awareness.

Safety and Accessibility:

- **Situational Awareness:** Be discreet with your gear, and understand your surroundings for safety.

- **Reputable Providers:** Vetting the tour company beforehand is crucial for ethical practices.

- **Fitness Level:** Consider how much walking, potential crowds, etc. the tour will involve.

Call to Action:

Ready to turn your lens into a tool for understanding the world? Explore photography tours with a storytelling twist!

55

Volunteer Vacationing

Volunteer Vacations: Travel with Purpose

Brief Description:

VOLUNTEER VACATIONS ALLOW YOU to combine the joy of travel with the opportunity to make a positive impact. Contribute your skills and time to meaningful projects in destinations around the world, fostering cultural exchange while exploring new places.

Why It's Great for Retirees:

- **Active Retirement:** Stay active and engaged while giving back to communities in need.

- **Skill Sharing:** Utilize your experience and knowledge in areas like teaching, construction, or healthcare.

- **Global Perspective:** Expand your worldview and gain a deeper understanding of different cultures.

- **Unique Travel Experiences:** Travel beyond tourist hotspots and connect with locals in a meaningful way.

Getting Started:

- **Identify Your Interests:** Choose a project that aligns with your skills and passions (education, wildlife conservation, community development).

- **Find a Reputable Program:** Research volunteer organizations that prioritize responsible practices and ethical project management.

- **Consider Time Commitment:** Programs range from short-term trips to longer-term commitments, choose what fits your schedule.

Resources Needed:

- **Open Mind and Flexibility:** Adapting to new environments and cultures is key to a successful volunteer experience.

- **Basic Language Skills:** Learning a few phrases in the local language goes a long way.

- **Physical Fitness:** Some programs may involve physical activity or working conditions that require good health.

Challenges and Tips:

- **Language Barriers:** Be prepared to communicate with limited language skills – patience and gestures can bridge the gap.

- **Cultural Adjustment:** Embrace differences, respect local customs, and be mindful of your impact.

- **Realistic Expectations:** Projects may not be glamorous, focus on the positive contribution you're making.

Ways to Deepen the Experience:

- **Immerse Yourself:** Homestay options or cultural activities can provide a deeper connection to the local community.

- **Learn a Local Skill:** Take a cooking class, participate in traditional crafts, or learn a new language.

- **Sustainable Volunteering:** Choose programs that prioritize responsible practices and community empowerment.

Safety and Accessibility:

- **Health Considerations:** Research necessary vaccinations and ensure your health insurance covers you abroad.

- **Program Reputation:** Choose established volunteer organizations with proven safety protocols and support structures.

- **Accessibility Options:** Many programs offer projects suitable for various physical abilities – inquire beforehand.

Call to Action:

Ready to combine travel with making a difference? Explore volunteer vacation opportunities and embark on a journey of purpose!

56

Astronomy Camps for Adults

Astronomy Camps for Adults: Reach for the Stars

Brief Description:

IMMERSE YOURSELF IN THE wonders of the cosmos at remote astronomy camps designed for adults. Experience the thrill of stargazing under pristine skies, learn from experts, and engage in fascinating discussions on the universe.

Why It's Great for Retirees:

- **Reignite Wonder:** Rediscover the awe-inspiring beauty of the night sky far from city lights.

- **Lifelong Learning:** Deepen your understanding of astronomy through workshops and lectures.

- **Connection & Camaraderie:** Meet like-minded individuals who share your passion for the cosmos.

- **Unique Travel Experience:** Venture off the beaten path to locations renowned for their dark skies.

Getting Started:

- **Beginner or Beyond:** Some camps cater to specific skill levels, from novice to experienced.

- **Scope or No Scope:** Choose camps with telescopes provided or those allowing you to bring your own.

- **Camp Style:** Lodging options range from basic campsites to comfortable cabins or retreats.

Resources Needed:

- **Enthusiasm for Learning:** Come ready to absorb new concepts and explore the universe.

- **Dark Sky Gear:** Warm clothing for nighttime sessions, red-light headlamps to protect night vision.

- **Astronomy Apps or Guides:** Help identify constellations, planets, and celestial objects.

Challenges and Tips:

- **Weather Dependence:** Stargazing can be impacted by clouds - have a flexible mindset.

- **Unfamiliar Territory:** Be prepared for rustic conditions in remote camp locations.

- **Steep Learning Curve:** If you're a beginner, be patient as you build your astronomy knowledge.

Ways to Deepen the Experience:

- **Astrophotography:** Learn how to capture stunning images of the night sky.

- **Guest Experts:** Some camps feature lectures by notable astronomers or space science experts.

- **Daytime Activities:** Explore the local area with hiking, birdwatching, or cultural excursions.

Safety and Accessibility:

- **Altitude Considerations:** Some camps are at high elevation, factor this into your health needs.

- **Camp Amenities:** Understand what facilities are provided (meals, bathrooms, accessibility options).

- **Camp Policies:** Inquire about light usage rules to protect everyone's dark sky experience.

Call to Action:

Are you ready to journey into the vastness of space? Discover astronomy camps for adults and unlock the secrets of the universe!

57

Archaeological Dig Vacations

Archaeological Dig Vacations: Unearth History, Layer by Layer

Brief Description:

BECOME PART OF AN active archaeological project, unearthing ancient artifacts and uncovering stories of past civilizations. Gain hands-on experience while contributing to ongoing research and the preservation of history.

Why It's Great for Retirees:

- **History Brought to Life:** Experience the thrill of discovery and see history firsthand.

- **Lifelong Learning:** Learn field techniques, excavation processes, and deepen your archaeological knowledge.

- **Travel with Purpose:** Explore fascinating destinations and contribute to preserving their cultural heritage.

- **Sense of Community:** Bond with fellow volunteers and professionals who share your passion for the past.

Getting Started:

- **Experience Needed:** Programs range from beginner-friendly to those requiring some prior knowledge.

- **Worldwide Destinations:** Choose digs based on your interests (Ancient Greece, Mayan ruins, etc.).

- **Dig Duration:** Options range from short programs to multi-week commitments.

Resources Needed:

- **Physical Fitness:** Excavation work can involve physical labor in varying climates.

- **Attention to Detail:** Archaeology requires meticulous observation skills and careful documentation.

- **Archaeological Guides:** Familiarize yourself with the site's historical context or brush up on terminology.

Challenges and Tips

- **The Unknown:** Be prepared for the unpredictable nature of archaeology – there might be major finds or quieter days.

- **Weather and Conditions:** Outdoor work exposes you to the elements, come prepared for heat, bugs, etc.

- **Patience is a Virtue:** Archaeological work is slow and precise, embrace the process.

Ways to Deepen the Experience:

- **Lectures and Workshops:** Augment your field experience with additional learning opportunities.

- **Museum Visits:** See artifacts from the site in a museum context for the full picture.

- **Cultural Excursions:** Explore the surrounding area for a deeper understanding of the society you're studying

Safety and Accessibility:

- **Camp Conditions:** Understand what accommodations are provided (tents, meals, healthcare access).

- **Vaccinations and Health:** Research what's required for the specific destination.

- **Project Leaders:** Choose reputable organizations with experienced archaeologists in charge.

Call to Action:

Ready to get your hands dirty in the name of history? Explore Archaeological Dig Vacations and help write the next chapter in our understanding of the past!

58

Culinary Exploration Tours

Culinary Exploration Tours: Taste the Heart of a Culture

Brief Description:

EMBARK ON A FLAVOR-FILLED adventure that reveals a destination's soul through its food. Go beyond restaurants with hands-on cooking classes, vibrant market explorations, and experiences that connect you to the source of local ingredients.

Why It's Great for Retirees:

- **Immersive Experience:** Food is a universal language, opening doors to authentic cultural exchange.

- **Expand Your Palate:** Discover new dishes, ingredients, and culinary traditions.

- **Passion Project:** Perfect for foodies or those seeking to deepen their culinary knowledge.

- **Memorable Souvenirs:** Bring home skills and recipes to recreate the flavors of your travels.

Getting Started:

- **Regional Focus:** Choose tours specializing in the cuisine you're passionate about (French, Thai, Mexican, etc.).

- **Skill Level:** Beginner-friendly to advanced cooking classes are available.

- **Beyond the Kitchen:** Seek tours that balance cooking with market visits, winery tours, etc.

Resources Needed:

- **Culinary Curiosity:** Come ready to try new things and explore beyond your comfort zone.

- **Foodie Notebook:** Record recipes, ingredients, and techniques you learn along the way.

- **Local Phrasebook:** Basic phrases help when shopping markets or interacting with locals.

Challenges and Tips:

- **Dietary Restrictions:** Inform tour operators beforehand to ensure accommodations can be made.

- **Pace Yourself:** Culinary tours can be packed with food experiences, savor each one!

- **Shopping Temptation:** Leave room in your luggage for spices, cookware, or foodie finds.

Ways to Deepen the Experience:

- **Farm or Producer Visits:** See where ingredients are grown, connecting the food to its origins.

- **Historical Foodie Walks:** Combine culinary exploration with historical sites related to the region's cuisine.

- **Unique Dining Experiences:** Seek out special meals cooked in traditional ways (home-cooked meals, etc.).

Safety and Accessibility:

- **Food Safety:** Reputable tours follow hygiene standards. Be cautious with street food if unsure.

- **Walking Tours:** Understand the pace and terrain of any included market or sightseeing walks.

- **Trusted Providers:** Look for operators who prioritize authentic experiences and food quality.

Call to Action:

Are your tastebuds ready for an adventure? Explore Culinary Exploration Tours and unlock the flavors of the world!

E-Bike Cycling Trips

E-Bike Cycling Trips: Conquer the Hills, Enjoy the Views

Brief Description:

Experience the joy of cycling without the limitations. E-bikes (electric bikes) provide a gentle boost, making scenic routes, stunning trails, and even challenging climbs accessible to all fitness levels.

Why It's Great for Retirees:

- **Rediscover Cycling:** Enjoy the freedom of two wheels, even if years have passed since your last ride.

- **No Sweat (Unless You Want It):** Choose how much effort you put in, tailoring the experience to your fitness goals.

- **Tackle Any Terrain:** Hills and longer distances are no longer a barrier with the assist of an e-bike.

- **Social Fun:** E-bikes let groups of varying abilities cycle together, keeping the focus on exploration.

Getting Started:

- **Guided vs. Self-Guided:** Tours provide logistics, while solo trips allow for ultimate flexibility.

- **Choosing Your Terrain:** Railtrails, coastal paths, country roads – the possibilities are endless.

- **Rentals or Bring Your Own:** Established e-bike destinations often offer top-line rentals.

Resources Needed:

- **Basic Bike Skills:** Steering, balance, and comfort on a bike are still needed.

- **E-Bike Intro:** A short tutorial on using the different power assist levels for a smooth ride.

- **Navigation:** Whether a tour guide or an app-route, know how you'll find your way.

Challenges and Tips:

- **Battery Range:** Understand your bike's limits and plan routes accordingly (especially for self-guided trips).

- **E-Bike Etiquette:** Be mindful on shared trails, as the extra speed needs awareness.

- **It's Still Exercise:** Even with assist, you'll be pedaling, so a base level of fitness helps.

Ways to Deepen the Experience:

- **Scenic Stops:** E-bikes let you go further, plan detours for viewpoints, charming villages, etc.

- **Foodie Focus:** Combine your e-bike tour with culinary adventures, refueling at local gems.

- **Multi-Sport Options:** Some tours include kayaking, hiking, etc., alongside the cycling.

Safety and Accessibility:

- **Helmet Laws:** Abide by local regulations and always choose to wear one while cycling.

- **Trail Conditions:** Ensure the route is suitable for your e-bike's style (road bike vs. mountain bike).

- **Tour Support:** Opt for guided tours with van support and mechanical knowledge for peace of mind.

Call to Action:

Ready to hit the open road with a little electric boost? Explore E-Bike Cycling Trips and see the world from a new perspective!

60

Mindfulness and Meditation Retreats

Mindfulness and Meditation Retreats: Find Stillness, Reconnect with Yourself

Brief Description:

ESCAPE THE BUSTLE OF daily life and embark on a transformative retreat focused on mindfulness, meditation, and holistic well-being. Experience a blend of guided meditations, yoga practices, and teachings designed to quiet the mind and cultivate inner peace.

Why It's Great for Retirees:

- **Combat Stress:** Learn techniques to manage stress and cultivate a greater sense of calm.

- **Self-Discovery:** Retreats offer time and space for reflection and personal growth.

- **Spiritual Exploration:** Many retreats offer a non-religious approach to mindfulness and spiritual connection.

- **Supportive Community:** Connect with like-minded individuals on a similar journey of self-care.

Getting Started:

- **Retreat Focus:** Choose themes that align with your needs (stress relief, beginner-friendly, specific meditation traditions).

- **Location and Setting:** From mountain monasteries to beachside resorts, the environment matters.

- **Silent vs. Interactive:** Some retreats are silent, others include group discussions and workshops.

Resources Needed:

- **Beginner's Mind:** An open mind and willingness to explore new practices are key.

- **Comfortable Clothing:** Yoga-friendly attire or loose clothes to enhance relaxation.

- **Meditation Aids:** If you have one, bring your cushion or bench, if not, most retreats provide them.

Challenges and Tips:

- **Disconnecting:** Unplugging from technology can be tough at first, but vital for the experience.

- **Emotional Release:** Meditation can surface deep emotions, embrace them as part of the process.

- **Integration Plan:** Consider how to bring mindfulness practices back into your daily life post-retreat.

Ways to Deepen the Experience:

- **Nature Immersion:** Choose retreats with outdoor meditation, mindful walks, or forest bathing.

- **Wellness Treatments:** Many retreats offer massage, acupuncture, or holistic therapies.

- **Healthy Cuisine:** Nourish your body with clean, often vegetarian meals to support your practice.

Safety and Accessibility:

- **Teacher Qualifications:** Research the background and experience of retreat leaders.

- **Health Considerations:** Inform the retreat center of any medical concerns or dietary restrictions.

- **Physical Requirements:** Inquire about the level of yoga or activities to ensure it's suitable.

Call to Action:

Ready to nurture your inner peace? Explore Mindfulness and Meditation Retreats and discover a more tranquil way of being.

61

Historic Railway Journeys

Historic Railway Journeys: Step Back in Time, Travel in Style

Brief Description:

EXPERIENCE THE GOLDEN AGE of train travel aboard lovingly restored historic railways. Indulge in opulent surroundings, breathtaking scenery, and the romance of a bygone era.

Why It's Great for Retirees:

- **Nostalgia Factor:** Recapture the charm and elegance of classic rail journeys.

- **Relaxed Pace:** Enjoy fine dining, leisurely scenery, and the chance to simply disconnect.

- **Unique Destinations:** Explore remote regions or iconic routes only accessible by these heritage lines.

- **Sense of Occasion:** Many journeys offer dress codes and themed experiences, adding to the allure.

Getting Started:

- **Iconic Trains:** Seek out legendary lines like the Orient Express, the Trans-Siberian, or the Rocky Mountaineer.

- **Global Journeys:** Each continent offers unique historic railways, from Africa to Australia.

- **Trip Duration:** Options range from short scenic jaunts to multi-day adventures.

Resources Needed:

- **Travel Documents:** Visas, passport validity, and any health requirements for your destination.

- **Elegant Attire:** Some journeys encourage dressing up, enhancing the vintage experience.

- **Nostalgia Resources:** Books or films about the railway's history can enrich your trip.

Challenges and Tips:

- **Cost:** Luxury and historic rail can be pricey. Research smaller lines for budget-friendlier options.

- **Limited Availability:** Popular journeys book up fast, plan in advance.

- **Pace of Travel:** While beautiful, the focus is on savoring the train ride itself, not whirlwind sightseeing.

Ways to Deepen the Experience:

- **Dress the Part:** Pack vintage-inspired outfits or embrace any themed nights onboard.

- **History Comes Alive:** Learn about the train's construction, routes, and famous passengers.

- **Off-Train Excursions:** Some journeys include stops at historic sites or cultural experiences.

Safety and Accessibility:

- **Train Accessibility:** Inquire about wheelchair access, onboard facilities, and any mobility limitations.

- **Destination Safety:** Research the safety and accessibility of places you'll disembark.

- **Reputable Providers:** Opt for established train operators with a commitment to passenger comfort and safety.

Call to Action:

Ready to indulge in a touch of travel history? Explore Historic Railway Journeys and embark on an unforgettable voyage!

62

Master Classes in Traditional Crafts

Master Classes in Traditional Crafts: Honor the Past, Shape Your Skills

Brief Description:

IMMERSE YOURSELF IN THE world of traditional crafts under the guidance of master artisans. Learn time-honored techniques like pottery, glassblowing, weaving, or other specialized crafts with a focus on preservation and mastery.

Why It's Great for Retirees:

- **Legacy Building:** Contribute to keeping traditional skills alive for future generations.

- **Creative Expression:** Discover new talents and explore your artistic side.

- **Sense of Accomplishment:** Create beautiful, handcrafted items with your own hands.

- **Community Connection:** Learn alongside others passionate about traditional crafts and their history.

Getting Started:

- **Choose Your Craft:** Explore your interests – pottery, woodworking, stained glass, the possibilities are vast.

- **Find a Master:** Seek out artisans known for their expertise and dedication to teaching.

- **Workshop Format:** Options range from one-day intensives to longer apprenticeships.

Resources Needed:

- **Dedication to Learning:** Mastering a traditional skill takes practice and commitment.

- **Workspace and Tools:** Some classes provide these, others require your own setup.

- **Source Guide:** Your instructor should offer guidance on where to find materials specific to your craft.

Challenges and Tips:

- **Patience and Practice:** Traditional techniques take time to master, enjoy the process.

- **Cost of Materials:** Some crafts have more specialized materials and tools than others, factor this in.

- **Physical Requirements:** Be aware of the physical demands of your craft (lifting, dexterity, etc.).

Ways to Deepen the Experience:

- **Historical Exploration:** Learn the origins and cultural significance of your chosen craft.

- **Visit Artisan Studios:** Observe experienced craftspeople in their element for inspiration.

- **Selling Your Work:** Explore craft fairs or online platforms to share your creations and support your art.

Safety and Accessibility:

- **Studio Safety:** Inquire about workshop safety guidelines and protective gear for your craft.

- **Health Considerations:** Some crafts involve dust, heat, or repetitive motions – be mindful if you have limitations.

- **Adaptive Tools:** Ask about options that may help with physical needs to make the craft more accessible.

Call to Action:

Are you ready to ignite your creative spirit and learn from the masters? Explore Master Classes in Traditional Crafts and embrace the satisfaction of creating something truly unique!

Learning and Education

63

Astronaut Training Experience for Seniors

Astronaut Training Experience for Seniors: Blast Off into Your Golden Years

Brief Description:

EVER DREAM OF BEING an astronaut? These programs tailor the thrilling experience of space travel for seniors. Participate in simulations, experience the feeling of zero-gravity, and gain insights into this extraordinary career path.

Why It's Great for Retirees:

- **Reignite Childlike Wonder:** Tap into the excitement of space exploration, regardless of age.

- **Unique Adventures:** Expand your horizons with an experience unlike any other.

- **Bonding Activity:** Share a memorable outing with friends, children, or grandchildren.

- **Educational and Inspiring:** Learn about the science and technology behind space travel.

Getting Started:

- **Look for Senior-Focused Programs:** Some facilities specifically tailor their astronaut experiences to older adults.

- **Fitness Level:** Understand the physical requirements, as some simulations might have limitations.

- **Accessibility:** Inquire about accommodations if you have any mobility restrictions.

Resources Needed:

- **Enthusiasm:** A thirst for adventure and a willingness to try new things are essential.

- **Comfortable Clothing:** Wear something easy to move in for the various activities.

- **Health Check:** Some programs may require a basic medical clearance for participation.

Challenges and Tips:

- **Potential for Motion Sickness:** Some simulations can induce motion sensitivity - be mindful.

- **Cost:** These specialty experiences can be a bit pricier than standard tours.

- **Fear Factor:** If heights or enclosed spaces make you anxious, ask about modifications.

Ways to Deepen the Experience:

- **Tour the Facility:** Combine your simulation experience with a full tour of a space center/museum.

- **Meet an Astronaut:** Some programs include talks or meet-and-greets with former astronauts.

- **Themed Extras:** Dress up in a spacesuit for fun photos to commemorate your adventure.

Safety and Accessibility:

- **Reputable Providers:** Prioritize programs run by established space centers or companies with safety expertise.

- **Age and Health Limits:** Be transparent about health conditions for suitability and potential adaptations.

- **Trained Staff:** Ensure supervisors are trained to assist seniors and address unexpected needs.

Call to Action:

Ready to reach for the stars? Explore Astronaut Training Experiences for Seniors and make your space travel dreams a reality!

64

Philosophy and Life's Big Questions

Philosophy and Life's Big Questions: Explore, Contemplate, Connect

Brief Description:

DELVE INTO LIFE'S MOST profound questions in a supportive group setting. Discuss philosophical concepts, grapple with big ideas, and gain new perspectives through thoughtful dialogue with others.

Why It's Great for Retirees:

- **Intellectual Stimulation:** Keep your mind sharp by engaging with complex and nuanced ideas

- **Community of Thinkers:** Connect with like-minded individuals passionate about exploring life's mysteries

- **Self-Discovery:** Philosophical discussions can offer profound insights into your own beliefs and values

- **No "Right" Answers:** Embrace open-ended questions and the joy of the exploration itself

Getting Started:

- **Finding Your Group:** Libraries, community centers, or online forums often host philosophy discussions.

- **Topic Focus:** Seek groups with themes that resonate (ethics, the meaning of life, etc.)

- **Facilitated vs. Open:** Some groups have a leader, others are free-flowing conversation

Resources Needed:

- **Curiosity and Open Mind:** Be receptive to diverse viewpoints and the challenge of abstract thinking.

- **Basic Background:** A quick brush-up on key philosophers or concepts can be helpful (online resources abound).

- **Respectful Debate:** Be willing to listen actively and engage in thoughtful disagreement.

Challenges and Tips:

- **Getting Deep:** It might take time to go beyond surface-level conversations – patience is key.

- **Diverse Viewpoints:** Embrace the challenge of perspectives that differ from your own.

- **Staying on Track:** Some groups benefit from a moderator to keep discussions focused.

Ways to Deepen the Experience:

- **Supplemental Readings:** Explore suggested texts by philosophers related to your group's focus.

- **Personal Journaling:** Record your reflections and questions sparked by the discussions.

- **Bridging the Gap:** Seek ways to apply philosophical concepts to your everyday life and decisions.

Safety and Accessibility:

- **Welcoming Environment:** Look for groups that emphasize respectful dialogue and inclusivity.

- **Virtual Options:** Online forums can be great if mobility or distance is a barrier.

- **Emotional Impact:** Be aware these discussions can sometimes touch on sensitive personal topics.

Call to Action:

Are you ready to embark on a journey of intellectual exploration? Seek out Philosophy and Life's Big Questions groups and start contemplating the wonders of existence!

65

Citizen Science Projects

Citizen Science Projects: Your Observations Power Real Research

Brief Description:

BECOME A PART OF the scientific community! Join citizen science projects where your observations and data collection directly contribute to ongoing research across various fields, from observing birds to monitoring water quality.

Why It's Great for Retirees:

- **Meaningful Contribution:** Use your time and skills to make a tangible difference in scientific understanding.

- **Lifelong Learning:** Explore new topics like astronomy, ecology, or meteorology.

- **Flexible Commitment:** Many projects offer varying participation levels to suit your availability.

- **Community Connection:** Collaborate with fellow citizen scientists and passionate researchers.

Getting Started:

- **Find Your Passion:** Explore online databases like SciStarter (https://scistarter.org/) to find projects that spark your interest.

- **Project Requirements:** Ensure the physical demands and time commitment align with your abilities.

- **Training Provided:** Most projects offer clear instructions, some even with online tutorials.

Resources Needed:

- **A Curious Mind:** Be eager to learn, observe, and follow project guidelines.

- **Basic Tech Skills:** Many projects involve online data entry or using smartphone apps.

- **Project-Specific Tools:** These might range from a simple notebook to specialized equipment (check project details).

Challenges and Tips:

- **Data Accuracy:** Prioritize careful observation and following project protocols for quality research.

- **Finding the Right Fit:** It might take trying a few projects to find one you truly connect with.

- **Limited Scope:** Understand your role is a piece of a larger research puzzle.

Ways to Deepen the Experience:

- **Go Beyond Data:** Read the project's findings to see how your contributions are used.

- **Local Connection:** Search for projects specifically focused on your region or environment.

- **Share the Joy:** Get friends or family involved, making it a collaborative activity.

Safety and Accessibility:

- **Virtual Options:** Many projects can be done entirely from your computer or phone.

- **Physical Considerations:** Choose fieldwork projects that align with your mobility and health.

- **Clear Instructions:** Projects should have well-defined safety protocols if hazards are present.

Call to Action:

Ready to put your curiosity to work? Explore the world of Citizen Science Projects and help unlock scientific discoveries!

66

Underwater Photography Courses

Underwater Photography Courses: Dive into a World of Creativity

Brief Description:

COMBINE THE THRILL OF scuba diving with specialized photography training. Learn to capture vibrant marine life, stunning shipwrecks, and the unique beauty of the underwater world.

Why It's Great for Retirees:

- **Exciting New Skills:** Master both scuba diving and the art of underwater photography.

- **Travel with Purpose:** Fuel your adventurous spirit by exploring stunning dive sites around the world.

- **Creative Expression:** Develop a unique artistic outlet and share the wonders of the ocean.

- **Fitness and Exploration:** Scuba diving offers physical benefits and a sense of discovery.

Getting Started:

- **Beginner or Advanced:** Look for courses tailored to your photography and diving experience levels.

- **Certification in One:** Many courses include Open Water Diver certification alongside photography.

- **Location and Focus:** Choose destinations based on the marine life or environments you wish to photograph.

Resources Needed:

- **Basic Swimming Skills:** Comfort in the water is essential for enjoying the course.

- **Underwater Camera:** Some courses offer rentals, while others require your own gear.

- **Dive Certification:** Required unless the course includes this alongside the photography training.

Challenges and Tips:

- **Multi-Tasking:** Balancing diving skills with camera operation requires practice and coordination.

- **Gear Expense:** Quality underwater camera equipment can be an investment tutorials.brentdurand.com

- **Patience is Key:** Capturing the perfect shot often means observing and waiting for marine life.

Ways to Deepen the Experience:

- **Marine Conservation:** Choose courses supporting conservation and ethical underwater photography.

- **Photo Editing Skills:** Learn post-processing techniques to enhance your underwater images.

- **Specialty Dives:** Expand your skills with wreck, night, or macro photography courses.

Safety and Accessibility:

- **Reputable Dive School:** Prioritize instructors with scuba and photography training expertise.

- **Health Considerations:** Scuba diving requires a certain level of fitness. Be transparent about any health conditions.

- **Buddy System:** Always dive in pairs or with an experienced guide for safety.

Call to Action:

Ready to capture the hidden wonders of our oceans? Explore Underwater Photography Courses and embark on a creative, aquatic adventure!

67

DIY Biohacking

DIY Biohacking: Explore, Experiment, Optimize (Safely!)

BRIEF DESCRIPTION: DISCOVER THE world of biohacking responsibly. These workshops guide you through basic biohacking concepts, from understanding your nutritional genetics to conducting safe, small-scale DIY biology experiments aimed at personal wellness.

Why It's Great for Retirees:

- **Personalized Health:** Learn how diet, lifestyle, and even your genes impact wellbeing.

- **Demystifying Science:** Hands-on workshops make concepts like DNA analysis more accessible.

- **Community and Support:** Connect with others interested in taking charge of their health.

- **Potential for Improvement:** Biohacking can offer insights to optimize sleep, nutrition, etc.

Getting Started:

- **Workshop Focus:** Choose your area of interest (nutrition, sleep optimization, fitness, etc.).

- **Reputable Instructors:** Seek leaders with scientific backgrounds and a focus on safety.

- **Realistic Expectations:** Biohacking won't cure all ailments, but can be part of a holistic approach.

Resources Needed:

- **Critical Thinking Skills:** Ability to analyze info and separate hype from valid science.

- **Lab Access:** Some workshops offer space and basic equipment, others assume you have your own.

- **Budget for Testing:** Genetic analysis, specialized supplements, etc., can incur costs.

Challenges and Tips:

- **Scientific Literacy:** A basic understanding of biology and chemistry is helpful.

- **Hype vs. Reality:** Be wary of overly-promising claims or instructors pushing specific products.

- **Self-Experimentation Risks:** Emphasize safety, start small, and consult healthcare professionals as needed.

Ways to Deepen the Experience:

- **Tracking and Data:** Measure and track your chosen metrics (sleep, blood sugar, etc.) before and after.

- **Holistic Approach:** Combine biohacking with established healthy lifestyle practices.

- **Sharing Responsibly:** If blogging about your experiences, emphasize safety and personal outcomes.

Safety and Accessibility:

- **Instructor Credentials:** Prioritize workshops led by qualified researchers or healthcare professionals.

- **Ethical Focus:** Avoid workshops encouraging unproven or potentially dangerous practices.

- **Informed Consent:** Good workshops clearly outline risks and emphasize personal choice.

Call to Action:

Ready to responsibly explore the possibilities of biohacking? Seek out DIY Biohacking Workshops that prioritize safety, science, and personal wellbeing!

Important Disclaimer:

DIY Biohacking can have risks. Consult your doctor before making significant changes to your health regimen, especially if you have underlying conditions.

68

Creative Writing Retreats

Creative Writing Retreats: Find Your Voice, Tell Your Story

Brief Description:

IMMERSE YOURSELF IN THE art of writing at a dedicated retreat. Enjoy the tranquility of inspiring locations, connect with fellow writers, and receive guidance from published authors to hone your craft.

Why It's Great for Retirees:

- **Focus and Motivation:** A retreat carves out distraction-free time for your writing projects.

- **Supportive Community:** Find camaraderie, feedback, and inspiration from fellow writers.

- **Expert Guidance:** Workshops with published authors enhance your writing skills and offer valuable insights.

- **Unlock Creativity:** Beautiful settings and structured writing time often ignite fresh ideas and perspectives.

Getting Started:

- **Genre Focus:** Choose retreats specializing in your interest (poetry, memoir, fiction, etc.).

- **Experience Levels:** Find retreats that cater to your skill level, from beginners to seasoned authors.

- **Location and Setting:** From mountain cabins to coastal villas, let the environment inspire you.

Resources Needed:

- **Your Work in Progress:** Bring existing writing or be prepared to start something new.

- **Laptop or Notebook:** Your preferred writing tools.

- **Openness to Feedback:** Be prepared to share your work and receive constructive criticism.

Challenges and Tips:

- **Performance Pressure:** Embrace the learning process and focus on personal growth, not perfection.

- **Balancing Structure and Free Time:** Some retreats are highly scheduled, others more relaxed.

- **Cost Factor:** Retreats can range in price - factor in accommodation, meals, and workshops.

Ways to Deepen the Experience:

- **Nature Immersion:** Choose retreats that incorporate outdoor time to inspire your writing.

- **Read and Reflect:** Bring works by favorite authors as inspiration and discussion points.

- **Post-Retreat Plan:** Set goals to keep the momentum going when you return home.

Safety and Accessibility:

- **Instructor Reputation:** Research the background and published works of the leading authors.

- **Venue Accessibility:** Ensure accommodations fit your mobility needs if applicable.

- **Emotional Safety:** Choose retreats fostering supportive environments for sharing personal writing.

Call to Action:

Ready to dive into a writing journey? Explore Creative Writing Retreats and let the words flow!

69

Indigenous Knowledge and Culture Programs

Indigenous Knowledge and Culture Programs: Learn, Connect, Honor Traditions

Brief Description:

IMMERSE YOURSELF IN THE rich history and living traditions of Indigenous communities. These programs offer a unique opportunity to learn directly about traditional ecological knowledge, sustainability practices, cultural art forms, and storytelling, fostering deeper understanding and respect.

Why It's Great for Retirees:

- **Expand Worldview:** Challenge preconceptions and gain new perspectives on history, land stewardship, and cultural preservation.

- **Authentic Experiences:** Learn directly from knowledge keepers within Indigenous communities.

- **Support and Preservation:** Your participation can aid efforts to preserve cultural heritage and languages.

- **Intergenerational Understanding:** Many programs bridge the gap between elders and youth, offering important insights.

Getting Started:

- **Focus Area:** Choose programs with themes that spark your curiosity (land management, arts, medicinal plants, etc.).

- **Respectful Providers:** Prioritize programs run by or in collaboration with Indigenous communities.

- **Commitment Level:** Options range from workshops to longer immersions.

Resources Needed:

- **Open Mind and Heart:** Be prepared to listen, learn, and unlearn with humility.

- **Cultural Protocols:** Your chosen program should clearly explain how to be a respectful visitor.

- **Physical Preparedness:** Some programs may involve outdoor activities – understand the requirements.

Challenges and Tips:

- **Overcoming Stereotypes:** Be aware of your own biases and the need for unlearning harmful narratives.

- **Emotional Impact:** Learning about the impacts of colonization can be difficult, but necessary.

- **Reciprocity:** Consider how you can give back (donations, skills, advocacy) beyond simply being a visitor.

Ways to Deepen the Experience:

- **Language Basics:** Learning a few phrases in the local Indigenous language shows respect.

- **Share Responsibly:** If blogging or sharing photos, do so with consent and context that uplifts the community.

- **Continued Learning:** Seek Indigenous authors, artists, and organizations to support beyond your program.

Safety and Accessibility:

- **Community-Centered:** Choose reputable programs with Indigenous communities' well-being at the forefront.

- **Accessibility Limitations:** Be transparent about any mobility or health needs when inquiring.

- **COVID-19 & Vulnerable Populations:** Understand precautions taken and potential risks, especially for elders

Call to Action:

Ready to embark on a journey of respect and learning? Explore Indigenous Knowledge and Culture Programs and play a small part in keeping these vital traditions alive.

Important Note:

Indigenous communities are diverse, with unique protocols and needs. The success of these programs relies on visitors prioritizing respect, seeking guidance, and understanding their role is to listen and learn.

70

Modern Art and Its Discontents

Modern Art and Its Discontents: Decipher, Debate, Discover

Brief Description:

DELVE INTO THE REVOLUTIONARY world of modern art movements, unraveling their complexities, historical context, and the controversies they often sparked. Engage in insightful lectures, thought-provoking museum visits, and lively discussions.

Why It's Great for Retirees:

- **Intellectual Engagement:** Challenge your artistic preconceptions and grapple with complex ideas.

- **Sharpen Critical Skills:** Learn to analyze modern artworks beyond simply liking or disliking them.

- **Cultural Exploration:** Move beyond the artwork itself to understand the social and political forces it reflects.

- **Connect with Like-mineds:** Share your evolving understanding with fellow art enthusiasts.

Getting Started:

- **Specific Movements:** Choose programs with a focus that intrigues you (Cubism, Dada, Pop Art, etc.).

- **Lecturer Expertise:** Prioritize programs led by art historians and experts in the chosen field.

- **Discussion-Based:** Seek out programs that encourage dialogue rather than just passive lectures.

Resources Needed:

- **Basic Art History:** A foundational knowledge of key art periods helps, but isn't strictly necessary.

- **Open to the Unfamiliar:** Be willing to encounter works that might challenge your initial taste.

- **Notebook and Pen:** Capture your observations, questions, and reactions during discussions.

Challenges and Tips:

- **Subjectivity in Art:** Embrace that there are no 'right' interpretations, and learn to articulate your own.

- **Demystifying Jargon:** Don't be intimidated by art-world terminology, ask for clarification.

- **Beyond the Gallery:** Do supplemental reading about the era to contextualize the art movements.

Ways to Deepen the Experience:

- **Artist Biographies:** Learn about the artists' lives, which often influenced their radical approach.

- **Comparative Explorations:** Look at artworks from different movements side-by-side for contrast.

- **Seek Out Modern Shows:** Continue your exploration by visiting local galleries and museums.

Safe and Accessible:

- **Learning Environment:** Choose a program that fosters respectful exploration for all knowledge levels.

- **Physical Accessibility:** Ensure museum visits and lecture locations are accessible to your needs.

- **Diverse Perspectives:** Programs benefit from including a range of viewpoints on the artwork

Call to Action:

Ready to dive into the complexities of modern art? Explore Programs focused on Modern Art and Its Discontents - you might be surprised by what you discover!

71

Wine and Cheese Making Classes

Wine and Cheese Making Classes: Craft Your Own Culinary Delights

Brief Description:

DISCOVER THE JOY OF artisanal food creation by learning the art and science of wine and cheese making. Explore fermentation, aging, flavor development, and the exciting interplay between these two culinary delights.

Why It's Great for Retirees:

- **Develop New Skills:** Transform ordinary ingredients into something remarkable with your own hands.

- **Farm-to-Table Connection:** Gain a deeper appreciation for handcrafted wines and cheeses.

- **Tasty Results:** Enjoy the fruits of your labor (literally!) and impress friends with your creations.

- **Social and Fun:** Many classes foster a sense of camaraderie while you get a bit messy!

Getting Started:

- **Beginner or Advanced:** Find classes tailored to your experience level, from basics to complex techniques.

- **Focus and Length:** Options range from one-day intensives to multi-week courses.

- **Your Choice:** Choose if you want to delve into wine, cheese, or both as a combo experience.

Resources Needed:

- **Instructor Guidance:** Good classes provide clear instructions and recipes to follow.

- **Starter Kits:** Classes often provide equipment, others assume you'll get a home kit.

- **Patience and Playfulness:** Fermentation takes time, and there's always room to experiment!

Challenges and Tips:

- **Space and Supplies:** Some cheeses/wines require aging space (temperature-controlled, etc.).

- **Initial Investment:** Specialized equipment and quality ingredients can have an upfront cost.

- **Failure as Learning:** Don't let less-than-perfect first batches discourage you – it's a skill to refine.

Ways to Deepen the Experience:

- **Pair and Share Night:** Host a tasting of your homemade creations for friends.

- **Visit Producers:** Go to a vineyard/cheesemaker to see the process on a larger scale.

- **Sensory Exploration:** Learn about flavor profiles and what makes pairings truly sing.

Safety and Accessibility:

- **Food Safety:** Especially with cheese, reputable classes prioritize hygiene and safe practices.

- **Alcohol Responsibility:** Be mindful of winemaking portions and enjoy responsibly.

- **Dietary Needs:** Inquire about vegan cheese-making options or alcohol-free winemaking alternatives.

Call to Action:

Unleash your inner winemaker and cheesemaker! Explore Wine and Cheese Making Classes and savor the delicious results.

72

Interactive History Experiences

Interactive History Experiences: Step Back in Time, Become Part of the Story

Brief Description:

IMMERSE YOURSELF IN HISTORY unlike ever before. Participate in reenactments, historical simulations, or explore detailed living history museums where you become part of a bygone era. Trade textbooks for time travel!

Why It's Great for Retirees:

- **Multi-Sensory Learning:** Engage all your senses – sights, sounds, even smells – for deeper understanding.

- **Social and Playful:** Bond with fellow participants, whether enacting roles or exploring a recreated world.

- **History Comes Alive:** Gain insights beyond facts, connecting emotionally to the struggles and triumphs of the past.

- **Discover Hidden Talents:** You might uncover a knack for period dancing or historical crafts!

Getting Started:

- **Choose Your Era:** From medieval battles to Victorian tea parties, let your curiosity guide you.

- **Participation Level:** Some events require full costume, others just a willingness to interact.

- **Family Friendly:** Many events welcome all ages, turning it into a multi-generational experience.

Resources Needed:

- **Period Appropriate Gear:** Some events provide this, others require you to source your own.

- **Basic Knowledge:** A bit of pre-event reading helps you jump right into the action.

- **Playful Spirit:** Embrace the chance to step outside yourself and into a different time.

Challenges and Tips:

- **Historical Accuracy:** Events vary in authenticity – do your research if this is important to you.

- **Comfort Zone:** Large-scale re-enactments can be chaotic and noisy – know your limits.

- **Physical Requirements:** Ensure the activities align with your abilities and mobility level.

Ways to Deepen the Experience:

- **Skills Workshops:** Learn traditional crafts or dances associated with your chosen era.

- **Behind the Scenes:** Volunteer to help set up, gaining further insight into the logistics of these events.

- **First-Person Accounts:** Seek out diaries or letters from people who lived through the period.

Safety and Accessibility:

- **Crowd Safety:** Large reenactments require awareness of your surroundings, especially with mock battles.

- **Accessibility Options:** Inquire about accommodations for those with mobility restrictions.

- **Inclusive Events:** Seek those that portray diverse historical roles and stories, not just dominant narratives.

Call to Action:

Ready to trade textbooks for a time-traveling adventure? Explore Interactive History Experiences and discover history in a whole new way!

Social and Cultural Activities

73

Literary Pilgrimages

Literary Pilgrimages: In the Footsteps of Literary Legends

Brief Description:

EMBARK ON A JOURNEY that blends travel with a love for literature. Visit the birthplaces, homes, and favorite writing spots of iconic authors. Immerse yourself in the landscapes and settings that sparked timeless classics, and partake in enriching discussions and readings amongst fellow book lovers.

Why It's Great for Retirees:

- **Deeper Appreciation:** Experience the environments that shaped an author's mind and stories.

- **Literary Connection:** Bond with like-minded individuals over a shared passion for the written word.

- **Enhanced Understanding:** Contextualize beloved books within the author's life and inspirations.

- **Travel with Purpose:** Discover hidden gems and off-the-beaten-path destinations linked to literary giants.

Getting Started:

- **Choose Your Author Focus:** From Shakespeare to Hemingway, let your literary passions guide you.

- **Organized Tours vs. DIY:** Tours offer expertise, while self-planning allows for ultimate flexibility.

- **Depth of Experience:** Select tours that incorporate readings, discussions, and visits to multiple locations.

Resources Needed:

- **The Author's Works:** Re-read or bring copies of the author's most famous pieces for on-location inspiration.

- **Biographies and Context:** Learn about the author's life to enrich your understanding.

- **Comfortable Walking Shoes:** Many literary pilgrimages involve exploring towns and homes on foot.

Challenges and Tips:

- **Off the Beaten Path:** Some destinations may be smaller villages less focused on mass tourism.

- **Prioritize the Experience:** Don't overload with too many locations, allow time to truly absorb each place.

- **Respectful Exploration:** Remember, even historical sites may be private homes still in use.

Ways to Deepen the Experience:

- **Local Connections:** Seek out pubs the author frequented or cafes known as literary gathering spots.

- **Creative Writing:** Use the surroundings to inspire your own poems, short stories, or journaling.

- **Themed Evenings:** Hold readings of your chosen author's works in evocative settings.

Safety and Accessibility:

- **Tour Group Support:** Organized tours often handle logistics and accessibility needs.

- **Rural Settings:** Be mindful of limited transportation options if visiting smaller sites independently.

- **Museum Accessibility:** Research access within the author's home or associated museums.

Call to Action:

Ready to follow in the footsteps of your favorite author? Explore Literary Pilgrimages and let their words guide you on a transformative adventure!

74

World Festival Tours

World Festival Tours: Immerse Yourself in Global Celebrations

Brief Description:

DIVE INTO THE HEART of global culture by joining a World Festival Tour. Immerse yourself in the electrifying atmosphere of iconic festivals, from the paint-filled revelry of India's Holi to the tomato-throwing La Tomatina in Spain. Gain a deeper understanding of local traditions and create unforgettable memories along the way.

Why It's Great for Retirees:

- **Cultural Exploration:** Experience traditions firsthand, gaining insights beyond what guidebooks can offer.

- **Adventure and Excitement:** Immerse yourself in the joyful chaos and energy of unique festivals.

- **Social Connection:** Mingle with locals and fellow travelers, forging new friendships.

- **Memorable Experiences:** Festivals offer vibrant spectacles and opportunities to step outside your comfort zone.

Getting Started:

- **Festival Focus:** Choose a tour based on a festival that sparks your curiosity (e.g., Carnival in Rio, Thailand's Loi Krathong).

- **Region or Theme:** Explore tours curated around specific regions or themes (e.g., South American cultural festivals, harvest festivals worldwide).

- **Tour Style:** Decide between small-group tours for a personalized experience or larger groups for a more social atmosphere.

Resources Needed:

- **Open Mind and Respect:** Be prepared to embrace cultural differences and participate with respect.

- **Comfortable Clothing and Footwear:** Dress for the specific climate and activities of the chosen festival.

- **Sense of Adventure:** Festivals can be lively and crowded – be willing to go with the flow.

Challenges and Tips:

- **Language Barriers:** Learn some basic phrases in the local language to enhance your experience.

- **Weather Conditions:** Research the typical weather during the festival to pack appropriately.

- **Responsible Participation:** Respect local customs and traditions, especially regarding religious festivals.

Ways to Deepen the Experience:

- **Pre-Trip Research:** Learn about the festival's history, rituals, and significance to the local culture.

- **Post-Festival Reflection:** Journal about your experiences and newfound cultural insights.

- **Support Local Artisans:** Purchase souvenirs from local vendors who help preserve cultural traditions.

Safety and Accessibility:

- **Tour Operator Reputation:** Choose reputable tour companies with a strong track record for safety and cultural sensitivity.

- **Physical Considerations:** Ensure your fitness level aligns with the demands of the festival activities.

- **Accessibility Options:** Inquire about accessibility features for tours and festival venues.

Call to Action:

Ready to celebrate the world's cultural tapestry? Explore World Festival Tours and embark on an unforgettable adventure filled with vibrant traditions, new connections, and a deeper appreciation for the world's diversity!

75

Opera and Symphony Behind-the-Scenes

Opera and Symphony Behind-the-Scenes: Witness the Magic Before the Curtain Rises

Brief Description:

STEP BEYOND THE VELVET seats and into the heart of the classical music world. Gain exclusive access to rehearsals, backstage tours, and meet-and-greets with talented musicians and opera singers. Observe the intricate preparation that goes into creating a world-class performance.

Why It's Great for Retirees:

- **Deeper Appreciation:** Witness the dedication and artistry required to bring music to life.

- **Exclusive Access:** Explore areas normally off-limits to the public, fostering a sense of privilege.

- **Connect with Musicians:** Engage with performers, gaining insights into their craft and passion.

- **Elevated Experience:** Enhance your enjoyment of future concerts with newfound knowledge.

Getting Started:

- **Opera Houses vs. Symphony Halls:** Choose experiences based on your preference.

- **Special Programs:** Many major performance venues offer behind-the-scenes tours or events.

- **Educational Focus:** Some experiences are geared towards deeper musical understanding.

Resources Needed:

- **Basic Music Knowledge:** Helps deepen your appreciation, but even novices can gain insights.

- **Comfortable Attire:** Dress code varies, but comfort and respect for the venue are key.

- **Keen Eye and Ear:** Be ready to observe complex staging elements and intricate musical details

Challenges and Tips:

- **Limited Availability:** These experiences may book up fast, plan in advance.

- **Observational Role:** You're mainly an observer, not an active participant in rehearsals.

- **Respect for Process:** Disruptions are a no-no, be prepared to be discreet and follow instructions.

Ways to Deepen the Experience:

- **Pre-Show Research:** Learn about the musical piece being rehearsed for richer context.

- **Post-Performance Reflection:** Attend a live performance afterward, noticing the details you observed.

- **Support Musicians:** Become a patron or donate to the organization to support their work.

Safety and Accessibility:

- **Backstage Logistics:** Be prepared for potentially tight spaces and uneven surfaces behind the scenes.

- **Accessibility Limitations:** Inquire about accommodations if you have mobility needs.

- **Tour Group Size:** Smaller groups often allow for more in-depth observation and interaction.

Call to Action:

Ready to peel back the curtain on the world of classical music? Explore Opera and Symphony Behind-the-Scenes experiences and let the music move you in a whole new way.

76

International Cooking Clubs

International Cooking Club: A Culinary Journey Around the World

Brief Description:

EXPAND YOUR PALATE AND culinary horizons with a vibrant community of food enthusiasts. Join our International Cooking Club, where we gather regularly to prepare and savor authentic dishes from across the globe. Embark on a flavor-filled adventure, occasionally guided by guest chefs who share their cultural expertise and cooking secrets.

*We add emphasis on the social aspect and the promise of learning from experts.

Why It's Great for Retirees:

- **Social Connection:** Combat loneliness and foster community over shared meals and a love of food.

- **Cultural Exploration:** Deepen your understanding of different cultures through their cuisine and food traditions.

- **Culinary Skills:** Develop new cooking techniques, experiment with exotic ingredients, and expand your recipe repertoire.

- **Fun and Festive:** Enjoy delicious meals in good company, creating joyful memories and sparking conversation.

Getting Started

- **Theme Selection:** Decide how to structure your culinary adventures - by country, region, specific dishes, etc.

- **Skill Levels Welcome:** Emphasize that both beginners and experienced cooks are encouraged to join.

- **Finding Guest Chefs:** Reach out to local restaurants, cultural centers, or even passionate home chefs within your community.

Resources Needed

- **Meeting Kitchen:** Ensure the space has adequate equipment and a comfortable dining area.

- **Specialty Ingredients:** Create a resource list for members to find less common ingredients.

- **Open Minds and Palates:** Be ready to step outside your comfort zone and taste new flavors!

Challenges and Tips

- **Ingredient Sourcing:** Plan ahead or provide a list of alternative ingredients if certain items are hard to find.

- **Dietary Restrictions:** Be mindful of allergies and food preferences, offering alternatives when possible.

- **Balance Expertise with Fun:** Guest chefs are a bonus, but keep the focus on a relaxed, collaborative cooking experience.

Ways to Deepen the Experience:

- **Cultural Presentations:** Ask members to share stories, music, or facts about the featured cuisine.

- **Hands-On Learning:** Focus on dishes that teach specific techniques (dumpling making, pasta rolling, etc.).

- **Themed Decorations:** Liven up the space and transport yourselves to the country of the day.

Safety and Accessibility

- **Kitchen Safety:** Review basic food safety and provide clear instructions for any complex dishes.

- **Mobility Considerations:** Choose kitchens with accessible layouts and adequate seating.

- **Communicate Clearly:** Ensure all members are aware of ingredients in advance to avoid allergies.

Call to Action:

Are you ready to embark on a global culinary journey? Join our International Cooking Club and let your taste buds take flight!

77

Artisanal Craft and Farmers Markets Road Trips

Artisanal Craft and Farmers Markets Road Trips: Explore, Discover, Support Local

Brief Description:

EMBARK ON A JOURNEY that celebrates craftsmanship and community. Our road trips take you off the beaten path to discover hidden gems: vibrant farmers markets and artisanal craft fairs. Connect with makers, sample farm-fresh flavors, and find unique treasures that tell a story.

Why It's Great for Retirees:

- **Purposeful Travel:** Turn a leisurely road trip into an adventure with a focus on supporting local economies.

- **Authentic Encounters:** Meet passionate artisans and farmers, hear their stories, and appreciate their skills.

- **Unexpected Finds:** Discover one-of-a-kind handmade goods, artisanal foods, and unique local specialties.

- **Slow Travel Vibe:** Savor the journey, explore charming towns, and enjoy the scenic routes between markets.

Getting Started:

- **Regional Focus:** Choose a specific region or state known for its craft and farming communities.

- **Market Calendars:** Plan your route and itinerary based on market dates and locations.

- **Mix and Match:** Combine bustling farmers markets with intimate craft fairs for a diverse experience.

Resources Needed:

- **Comfortable Vehicle:** Ensure sufficient space to bring back your newfound treasures.

- **Local Resources:** Utilize online directories and tourism websites to find markets in your chosen area.

- **Cooler and Tote Bags:** Keep your fresh produce and perishable purchases safe for the trip.

Challenges and Tips:

- **Seasonality:** Some markets are seasonal, so plan your trip according to the region's harvest times.

- **Cash is King:** Many smaller vendors may not accept cards, so be prepared with cash on hand.

- **Leave Room in the Trunk:** It's easy to be tempted by beautiful crafts and delicious finds!

Ways to Deepen the Experience:

- **Farm Tours:** If available, combine market visits with tours of local farms to see where your food comes from.

- **Artisan Workshops:** Some markets offer demonstrations or workshops, allowing you to try your hand at a craft.

- **Local Flavor:** Dine at farm-to-table restaurants and explore the region's culinary specialties.

Safety and Accessibility:

- **Market Hours:** Verify market days and hours of operation in advance to avoid disappointment.

- **Navigating Crowds:** Some popular markets can get crowded, be mindful of your pace and surroundings.

- **Food Safety:** Exercise caution with food samples, especially if you have food sensitivities.

Call to Action:

Ready to hit the road and discover the heart of local communities? Explore Artisanal Craft and Farmers Market Road Trips for an adventure filled with unique finds and meaningful connections.

78

Silent Reading Parties

Discover the Joy of Shared Reading

Brief Description:

REDISCOVER THE SIMPLE PLEASURE of reading in a social setting. Join our Silent Reading Parties, where we gather in inspiring locations to immerse ourselves in our current reads. Enjoy the camaraderie of fellow book lovers, followed by lively discussions about what's captured our imaginations.

Why It's Great for Retirees:

- **Dedicated Reading Time:** Carve out a distraction-free space to reconnect with the written word.

- **Social without Pressure:** Enjoy the company of other readers without the need for constant small talk.

- **Bookish Inspiration:** Discover new authors and genres based on what others are reading.

- **Community Connection:** Bond with like-minded individuals over shared literary experiences.

Getting Started:

- **Cozy Locations:** Choose comfortable spots with minimal noise – libraries, cafes, parks, even beautiful homes!

- **Set Reading Time:** Decide on a dedicated reading period (60-90mins is ideal), with discussion after.

- **No Assigned Books:** Encourage everyone to bring their current, personal choice of read.

Resources Needed:

- **Your Favorite Book:** The only essential "equipment" for this gathering.

- **Comfortable Seating:** Cushions, blankets, or your favorite reading chair.

- **Optional Beverage:** Tea, coffee, or something simple to enhance the cozy atmosphere.

Challenges and Tips:

- **Finding Quiet Spots:** Scout locations in advance to ensure they're conducive to focused reading.

- **Respecting Introverts:** Discussion is encouraged, but never pressured – some just love the quiet reading time.

- **Diverse Tastes:** Don't be discouraged if everyone's books are different, that makes the discussion richer!

Ways to Deepen the Experience:

- **Themed Selections:** Occasionally suggest a theme (nature writing, short stories, etc.) for focused discovery.

- **Local Bookstore Tie-In:** Partner with a bookstore for discounts or to have staff lead occasional discussions.

- **Beyond Books:** If the group bonds, transition to sharing magazines, poetry or long form articles as well.

Safety and Accessibility:

- **Venue Accessibility:** Ensure the location is accessible for all members of your group.

- **Lighting and Noise:** Choose well-lit, quiet areas to minimize strain and aid concentration.

- **Respectful Volume:** Keep book discussions at a respectful volume to avoid disrupting others nearby.

Call to Action:

Ready to lose yourself in a good book and connect with fellow bibliophiles? Seek out or start a Silent Reading Party in your area and experience the joy of reading together!

79

Cultural Exchange Dinner Parties

Cultural Exchange Dinner Parties: A Culinary Journey Around the World

Brief Description:

EXPAND YOUR HORIZONS AND tantalize your taste buds! Join our Cultural Exchange Dinner Parties, where we embark on a culinary adventure to different countries each gathering. Savor authentic dishes, share stories, and immerse yourself in vibrant traditions – all from the comfort of your own dining room.

Why It's Great for Retirees:

- **Travel Through Food:** Experience the world's diverse cultures without ever leaving home.

- **Learning and Connection:** Deepen your understanding of different traditions through shared meals and meaningful conversations.

- **Culinary Exploration:** Discover new flavors, recipes, and cooking techniques.

- **Fostering Community:** Build friendships with a shared interest in global cultures and cuisines.

Getting Started:

- **Theme Selection:** Rotate through countries, regions, or even specific celebrations (holidays, festivals, etc.).

- **Collaborative Menu:** Participants can volunteer to prepare a dish or contribute drinks/snacks.

- **Beyond the Food:** Encourage guests to bring a short presentation, music, or photos relating to the featured culture.

Resources Needed:

- **A Love of Food:** A willingness to try new things and experiment in the kitchen... or simply an appetite for adventure!

- **Themed Resources:** Basic recipes, music playlists, or talking points about the featured culture.

- **Open Minds and Welcoming Hearts:** The most important ingredients for a successful gathering.

Challenges and Tips:

- **Dietary Needs:** Accommodate food restrictions to ensure everyone feels included.

- **Research Depth:** Balance fun facts with respect for the culture; avoid stereotypes or oversimplification.

- **Potluck Logistics:** If sharing dishes, have a plan for serving, food labeling, and ensuring a balanced meal.

Ways to Deepen the Experience:

- **Dress the Part (Optional):** Add a festive element by encouraging guests to wear traditional attire.

- **Language Lesson:** Teach each other a few key phrases from the featured country.

- **Charity Component:** Support charities related to the chosen culture through donations or volunteering.

Safety and Accessibility:

- **Ingredient Transparency:** Clearly label dishes for those with allergies or dietary restrictions.

- **Inclusive Atmosphere:** Ensure the space is welcoming to guests of all backgrounds and abilities.

- **Mindful Portions:** Offer small portions to allow tasting of multiple dishes without waste.

Call to Action:

Ready to turn your dinner table into a passport to global discovery? Join or start a Cultural Exchange Dinner Party and savor the world one delicious bite at a time!

80

Classic Film Series and Discussion

Classic Film Series: Journey Through Cinematic History

Brief Description:

REDISCOVER THE MAGIC OF timeless cinema and engage in insightful discussions. Our Classic Film Series invites you to delve into masterpieces from various eras and countries. We'll screen iconic films followed by lively conversations exploring their artistic merit, historical context, and enduring cultural impact.

Why It's Great for Retirees:

- **Film as Art:** Reawaken your appreciation for the artistry and storytelling power of classic cinema.

- **Intellectual Stimulation:** Challenge yourself with new perspectives and engage in thoughtful analysis.

- **Social and Nostalgic:** Bond with fellow film enthusiasts, reminiscing and sharing interpretations.

- **Expanding Horizons:** Discover hidden gems and explore diverse genres or international film movements.

Getting Started:

- **Curated Selections:** Create themes (Golden Age Hollywood, Film Noir, Italian Neorealism, etc.).

- **Sourcing Films:** Utilize libraries, streaming services, or partner with a local cinema if possible.

- **Discussion Leaders:** Knowledgeable moderators can guide conversation, but audience participation is key.

Resources Needed:

- **Screening Space:** A comfortable venue with good projection and sound (library meeting room, home theater, etc.).

- **Background Materials:** Brief film synopses, historical context, or discussion prompts for participants.

- **Passion for Film:** A love of movies and the desire to dig deeper into their meaning.

Challenges and Tips:

- **Diverse Voices:** Encourage participants with various film knowledge to contribute and learn from each other.

- **Respectful Debate:** Foster an open space where differing opinions are explored respectfully.

- **Spoilers Alert:** Be mindful of first-time viewers, perhaps have a brief 'spoiler free' discussion section.

Ways to Deepen the Experience:

- **Guest Speakers:** Invite film scholars or historians for special screenings and lectures.

- **Themed Extras:** Period-appropriate snacks, or dress in the style of the film's era for a fun touch.

- **Further Exploration:** Create a resource list with related books, documentaries, or similar films.

Safety and Accessibility:

- **Comfortable Venue:** Ensure adequate seating, lighting, and good sound for all participants.

- **Hearing Assistance:** Inquire about assistive listening devices or closed captioning options if needed.

- **Film Runtime:** Be mindful of film length for comfort, and allow for breaks as needed.

Call to Action:

Ready to embark on a cinematic journey of discovery and discussion? Join our Classic Film Series and experience the enduring power of movies!

81

Eco-tourism and Conservation Safaris

Eco-tourism and Conservation Safaris: Explore, Learn, and Contribute

Brief Description:

EMBARK ON AN ECO-CONSCIOUS adventure into nature reserves and conservation areas. Led by expert guides, discover diverse wildlife in their natural habitats, learn about conservation challenges, and understand how sustainable tourism directly supports these efforts.

Why It's Great for Retirees:

- **Purposeful Travel:** Combine a love for nature with a desire to make a positive impact on the planet.

- **Educational Immersion:** Gain in-depth insights into fragile ecosystems, conservation efforts, and local wildlife.

- **Ethical Encounters:** Observe animals responsibly, ensuring your presence benefits their protection.

- **Support Sustainable Practices:** Your participation contributes to the long-term health of the environment and local communities.

Getting Started:

- **Destination Choice:** Select regions known for ecotourism: Africa, Costa Rica, the Galapagos Islands, etc.

- **Reputable Operators:** Seek companies committed to minimal impact, local guides, and conservation funding.

- **Wildlife Focus:** Safaris can specialize in specific animals (big cats, primates, marine life) or overall biodiversity.

Resources Needed:

- **Respectful Mindset:** Prioritize the well-being of the environment and wildlife above all else.

- **Physical Preparedness:** Understand the fitness level required (walking, early mornings, basic accommodations).

- **Photography Gear (Optional):** Capture stunning wildlife images while adhering to ethical guidelines.

Challenges and Tips:

- **Cost Factor:** Eco-tourism can be more expensive, but reflects your investment in a worthy cause.

- **Leave No Trace:** Follow strict guidelines to minimize your footprint on the environment.

- **Patience is Key:** Wildlife sightings are thrilling but not guaranteed – embrace the journey of observation.

Ways to Deepen the Experience:

- **Conservation Talks:** Attend lectures on-site to gain a broader understanding of environmental issues.

- **Local Engagement:** Learn about community-based conservation initiatives and how tourism helps them.

- **Post-Trip Action:** Become an advocate for the region, supporting conservation organizations back home.

Safety and Accessibility:

- **Health and Safety:** Consult with your doctor and research any required vaccinations for your destination.

- **Reputable Outfitters:** Choose operators with clear safety protocols and emergency plans.

- **Physical Limitations:** Inquire about tour options that accommodate various fitness and mobility levels.

Call to Action:

Ready to make your travels meaningful? Explore Eco-tourism and Conservation Safaris and play an active role in protecting our planet's precious wildlife!

82

Life Memoir Writing Workshops

Life Memoir Writing Workshops: Capture Your Story, Leave Your Legacy

Brief Description:

REDISCOVER THE RICHNESS OF your life's journey and preserve your unique story for generations to come. Our memoir writing workshops provide a structured, supportive environment to reflect, write, and share your experiences.

Why It's Great for Retirees:

- **Self-Discovery & Reflection:** Gain new perspectives on your past and uncover the meaning within your memories.

- **Legacy Building:** Create a priceless gift for your family and loved ones, sharing your wisdom and values.

- **Therapeutic Benefits:** Find healing and closure through the process of revisiting and writing about your experiences.

- **Community Connection:** Bond with others on a similar journey of self-expression and sharing stories.

Getting Started:

- **Workshop Format:** Choose between multi-session courses or focused weekend intensives.

- **Instructor Guidance:** Look for workshops led by experienced writers or facilitators skilled in memoir writing.

- **No Writing Experience Needed:** These workshops welcome all levels, with the emphasis on the journey, not just the final product.

Resources Needed:

- **Memory Prompts:** Exercises, questions, and old photos can help spark your recollections.

- **Notebook or Laptop:** Dedicated space to record your thoughts and drafts.

- **Willingness to Share:** Be prepared to open up with the group, offering and receiving constructive feedback.

Challenges and Tips:

- **Emotional Moments:** It's okay if writing stirs up emotions, the workshop offers support and guidance.

- **Finding Your Voice:** Don't worry about perfect grammar initially, focus on capturing your authentic voice.

- **The Power of Details:** Sensory details bring your stories to life for a reader.

Ways to Deepen the Experience:

- **Guest Speakers:** Published memoirists can offer inspiration and practical publishing advice (if desired).

- **Themed Workshops:** Focus on specific life stages (childhood, career, major life events).

- **Legacy Project:** Option to create a bound keepsake of participants' selected writings at the course end.

Safety and Accessibility:

- **Supportive Environment:** Emphasis on a non-judgmental space where everyone's stories are valued.

- **Sharing Comfort Levels:** Participants control how much they share at each stage of the process.

- **Accessibility Options:** Ensure venue is accessible and inquire about online workshops if needed.

Call to Action:

Ready to embark on a journey of self-discovery and preserve your unique life story? Explore Life Memoir Writing Workshops and start writing your own extraordinary chapters!

Personal Development

83

Mindfulness and Resilience Retreats

Mindfulness and Resilience Retreats: Find Inner Calm, Cultivate Strength

Brief Description:

ESCAPE THE STRESSES OF daily life and nurture your emotional well-being. Our retreats offer a peaceful sanctuary to learn mindfulness techniques, practice gentle yoga, and participate in workshops that enhance your ability to cope with life's challenges.

Why It's Great for Retirees:

- **Stress Reduction:** Learn tools to manage stress and cultivate a greater sense of peace in everyday life.

- **Mindful Aging:** Develop strategies to navigate transitions and embrace changes with a sense of calm.

- **Emotional Resilience:** Build inner strength to better handle unexpected situations and life's inevitable challenges.

- **Supportive Community:** Connect with like-minded individuals in a safe and nurturing environment.

Getting Started:

- **Retreat Focus:** Choose themes aligned with your needs (stress management, grief support, finding purpose, etc.).

- **Experience Levels:** Find retreats catering to beginners or those with existing mindfulness practices.

- **Location and Setting:** Mountain monasteries, seaside retreats, or cozy wellness centers all offer different vibes.

Resources Needed:

- **Comfortable Clothing:** Yoga-appropriate wear and layers for various activities.

- **Open Heart and Mind:** Willingness to explore new techniques and reflect on your inner self.

- **Journal or Notebook:** Capture insights from workshops and guide your personal reflections.

Challenges and Tips:

- **Disconnecting:** Leave your phone behind (if safe) to truly immerse yourself in the experience.

- **Gentle Approach:** Honor your body's limitations, especially if yoga is new to you.

- **Post-Retreat Plan:** Bring the mindfulness tools learned back into your daily life for lasting impact.

Ways to Deepen the Experience:

- **Nature Immersion:** Choose retreats with outdoor meditation, mindful walks, and time to simply 'be' in nature.

- **Nourishing Meals:** Whole-food, plant-forward cuisine supports your overall sense of well-being.

- **Therapists On-Site (Optional):** Some retreats offer individual counseling for deeper personal work.

Safety and Accessibility:

- **Instructor Qualifications:** Seek retreats with certified yoga teachers and workshop leaders with mental health expertise.

- **Physical Limitations:** Inquire about modifications and if the venue is fully accessible.

- **Emotional Safety:** Emphasize a trauma-informed approach and respect for participants' comfort levels when sharing.

Call to Action:

Ready to invest in your emotional well-being? Explore Mindfulness and Resilience Retreats and discover the inner peace and strength you carry within.

84

Digital Legacy Planning

Digital Legacy Planning: Secure Your Online Presence, Preserve Your Story

BRIEF DESCRIPTION: NAVIGATE THE complexities of your digital footprint with our practical workshops. Learn how to manage social media accounts, online assets, and important documents. Ensure your digital legacy is secure, reflects your wishes, and protects your loved ones.

Why It's Great for Retirees:

- **Peace of Mind:** Gain control over your digital presence and make informed decisions about its future.

- **Protect Your Loved Ones:** Avoid confusion and potential conflicts by clearly outlining your digital legacy plans.

- **Preserve What Matters:** Safeguard precious online memories, photos, and creative works for future generations.

- **Tech Empowerment:** Workshops break down complex concepts, empowering you to manage your digital world.

Getting Started:

- **Workshop Scope:** Options range from basic overviews to in-depth sessions on specific platforms or assets.

- **Inventory Your Footprint:** Before the workshop, list your accounts, online subscriptions, and digital possessions.

- **Instructor Expertise:** Seek workshops led by tech-savvy facilitators with an understanding of estate planning issues.

Resources Needed:

- **List of Accounts and Passwords:** You may be taught about secure password managers for organization.

- **Questions and Concerns:** Prepare specific questions about platforms or assets you want help with.

- **Device (Optional):** Some workshops might have hands-on elements where bringing a laptop could be useful.

Challenges and Tips:

- **Updating Plans:** Digital landscapes change, so revisit your legacy plan regularly.

- **Security First:** Learn about password best practices, multi-factor authentication, and avoiding scams.

- **Trusted Person:** Designate a tech-savvy loved one or professional to carry out your digital legacy wishes.

Ways to Deepen the Experience:

- **Guest Experts:** Invite estate planning attorneys to address the legal side of digital assets.

- **Focus on Sentimentality:** Include discussions on curating online photo albums or meaningful social media posts.

- **Family Workshops:** Offer sessions for multiple generations to work on digital legacy planning together.

Safety and Accessibility:

- **Reputable Providers:** Libraries, senior centers, or tech companies often offer these workshops.

- **Clear Communication:** Instructors should avoid jargon and offer step-by-step guidance.

- **Individual Support:** Option for follow-up consultations for those needing extra assistance.

Call to Action:

Take charge of your digital legacy! Explore Digital Legacy Planning workshops and ensure your online life is secure, organized, and reflects your values.

85

Adventure-Based Learning Experiences

Adventure-Based Learning Experiences: Embrace Challenge, Ignite Your Spirit

Brief Description:

STEP OUT OF YOUR comfort zone and tap into your untapped potential. Our adventure learning experiences combine exhilarating activities like sailing, mountaineering, or wilderness exploration with expert guidance and skill development. Rediscover your strength, resilience, and the joy of conquering new challenges.

Why It's Great for Retirees:

- **Physical and Mental Boost:** Push your limits in a safe environment, building strength, confidence, and adaptability.

- **New Skills, New Horizons:** Master the basics of a thrilling new sport or outdoor activity.

- **Community and Shared Challenge:** Bond with like-minded adventurers, supporting each other's growth.

- **Reignite Your Spark:** Break free from routine and inject a sense of excitement and purpose into your life.

Getting Started:

- **Choose Your Thrill:** Consider your interests and fitness level - sailing, rock climbing, kayaking, etc.

- **Experience vs. Expertise:** Many programs welcome beginners, with a focus on safe, progressive learning.

- **Location, Location:** Explore breathtaking destinations, from coastal adventures to mountain expeditions.

Resources Needed:

- **Adventurous Spirit:** A willingness to try, a touch of grit, and a good sense of humor!

- **Appropriate Gear:** Programs provide specialized equipment, but some basics may be yours to source.

- **Health Check-Up:** Consult your doctor, especially for more physically demanding adventures.

Challenges and Tips:

- **Gradual Progression:** Programs cater to various levels, start with a challenge that excites, but doesn't overwhelm.

- **Listen to Your Body:** Honor your limits while also gently pushing yourself to grow.

- **Celebrate Every Milestone:** Focus on the journey, not just the summit. It's about self-discovery, not competition.

Ways to Deepen the Experience:

- **Mindfulness Component:** Incorporate reflection time to process the link between physical and mental challenge.

- **Adventure Journaling:** Document your experience, the highs and even the lows, for future inspiration.

- **Photographic Focus:** Capture the beauty of the landscape and the camaraderie of your group.

Safety and Accessibility:

- **Reputable Providers:** Prioritize programs with experienced instructors and a strong safety track record.

- **Inclusive Options:** Seek adventures with varying intensity levels or adaptive equipment if needed.

- **Transparency About Demands:** Ensure the program is clear about the expected physical requirements.

Call to Action:

Ready to unleash your adventurous side? Explore Adventure-Based Learning Experiences and prove to yourself that age is just a number!

86

Ethical Living Workshops

Ethical Living Workshops: Align Your Actions with Your Values

Brief Description:

DISCOVER PRACTICAL WAYS TO live a more ethical and sustainable life. Our workshops offer guidance on eco-friendly choices, mindful consumption, ethical investing, and ways to create positive change in your community and the world.

Why It's Great for Retirees:

- **Live with Purpose:** Turn your desire for a better world into concrete actions that make a difference.

- **Informed Choices:** Gain the knowledge to make ethical decisions regarding your finances, purchases, and lifestyle.

- **Combat Eco-Anxiety:** Feel empowered by learning tangible steps to reduce your environmental impact.

- **Legacy Building:** Leave a lighter footprint for future generations and inspire others to do the same.

Getting Started:

- **Focus Area:** Choose workshops covering broad ethical living or a specific topic (zero-waste home, fair trade, etc.).

- **Action-Oriented:** Prioritize workshops that provide practical tips and resources, not just theory.

- **Local Expertise:** Look for facilitators with connections to ethical businesses and initiatives in your region.

Resources Needed:

- **Open Mind:** Be willing to examine your habits and consider new approaches.

- **Notebook:** Record key takeaways, resources, and action steps you want to implement.

- **Community Spirit:** Share your successes and challenges with the group for support.

Challenges and Tips:

- **Avoiding 'Greenwashing':** Workshops should teach how to spot misleading environmental claims.

- **Imperfect Progress:** Emphasize that every positive change matters, perfection isn't the goal.

- **Affordability:** Discuss budget-friendly ways to make ethical shifts in your life

Ways to Deepen the Experience:

- **Guest Speakers:** Local business owners demonstrating ethical practices can be inspiring.

- **Group Action Project:** Work together on a community initiative (cleanup drive, petition, etc.).

- **Follow-Up Resources:** Provide curated lists of ethical brands, organizations, and further learning.

Safety and Accessibility:

- **Inclusive Environment:** Ensure the workshop welcomes diverse perspectives and financial situations.

- **Avoid Doomscrolling:** Balance learning about the problems with a strong focus on solutions.

- **Accessibility:** Choose venues accommodating a range of mobility needs and offer online options.

Call to Action:

Ready to make your daily life a reflection of your values? Explore Ethical Living Workshops and discover the power of living in alignment with your conscience.

87

Intergenerational Learning Programs

Intergenerational Learning Programs: Share Knowledge, Build Bridges, Grow Together

Brief Description:

BREAK DOWN GENERATIONAL BARRIERS and discover the joy of cross-generational connection. Our programs pair retirees with younger individuals for mutual learning and mentoring. Share your life experience, wisdom, and skills, while staying current with the latest trends and perspectives.

Why It's Great for Retirees:

- **Combat Isolation:** Build meaningful friendships across generations and feel valued for your contributions.

- **Stay Sharp:** Learning from younger generations keeps your mind active and engaged with the changing world.

- **Legacy Building:** Pass on your knowledge, traditions, and stories to ensure they live on.

- **Gain New Skills:** From tech help to fresh perspectives, tap into the knowledge and energy of youth.

Getting Started:

- **Program Format:** Choose between structured mentorship, informal skill swaps, or storytelling sessions.

- **Your Passion:** Focus on areas where you can genuinely teach and learn (technology, crafts, career advice).

- **Open to Difference:** Embrace diverse viewpoints and backgrounds – the key is the willingness to connect.

Resources Needed:

- **Empathy and Patience:** Focus on building relationships, the knowledge exchange will follow organically.

- **Designated Space:** Programs might have meeting rooms or facilitate online connections if needed.

- **Shared Activity (Optional):** Having a project (community garden, oral history) makes it less about the age gap.

Challenges and Tips:

- **Scheduling Conflicts:** Flexible programs work best with retirees' schedules and young people's commitments.

- **Finding the Right Match:** Good programs consider personalities, not just skill sets, when pairing participants.

- **Mutual Respect:** Emphasize that both generations are teachers and both are learners.

Ways to Deepen the Experience:

- **Community Events:** Showcase the results of intergenerational collaboration (performances, exhibits, etc.).

- **Celebrating Differences:** Include sessions focused on how each generation's experience shapes their outlook.

- **Long-Term Potential:** Option for pairs who connect well to continue a mentoring relationship on their own.

Safety and Accessibility:

- **Background Checks:** Especially if working with minors, programs must prioritize safety.

- **Inclusive Environment:** Ensure diverse participants feel welcome (race, LGBTQ+, disability accommodations).

- **Conflict Mediation:** Facilitators should be trained to handle any misunderstandings that might arise.

Call to Action:

Ready to enrich your life and the lives of others? Explore Intergenerational Learning Programs and discover the power of connection across generations!

88

Personal Finance and Legacy Planning

Personal Finance and Legacy Planning: Secure Your Future, Leave Your Mark

Brief Description:

NAVIGATE THE COMPLEXITIES OF retirement finances and create a meaningful legacy that reflects your values. Our seminars offer expert guidance on managing investments, estate planning essentials, and strategic philanthropy to maximize your impact.

Why It's Great for Retirees:

- **Peace of Mind:** Gain clarity and control over your long-term financial well-being.

- **Informed Decisions:** Understand the options available for protecting and distributing your assets.

- **Protect Loved Ones:** Ensure your wishes are honored and your family is provided for after you're gone.

- **Purposeful Giving:** Learn how to make your philanthropy effective and aligned with your passions.

Getting Started:

- **Seminar Focus:** Choose between broad overviews or deep dives into specific topics (trusts, tax implications, etc.).

- **Reputable Professionals:** Seek seminars led by certified financial planners and estate planning attorneys.

- **Your Questions:** Prepare a list of specific concerns you have, big or small, to get the most out of sessions.

Resources Needed:

- **Basic Financial Records:** A general overview of your assets and debts can aid in tailored advice.

- **Notebook or Device:** To record important information and resources shared during the seminar.

- **Open to Collaboration:** Be receptive to potentially partnering with professionals for personalized plans.

Challenges and Tips:

- **Avoid Sales Pitches:** Prioritize seminars focused on education over selling specific products.

- **Plain Language:** Instructors should break down complex jargon and provide real-world examples.

- **Emotional Component:** Acknowledge that legacy planning can stir up difficult emotions, offering support resources if needed.

Ways to Deepen the Experience:

- **Case Studies:** Analyze anonymized examples of successful legacy plans for inspiration and insights.

- **Philanthropy Spotlight:** Invite local charities to briefly share how planned giving impacts their work.

- **Q&A Time:** Ample opportunity to address individual questions and receive targeted guidance.

Safety and Accessibility:

- **Fee Transparency:** Upfront clarity about seminar costs and if consultations have further fees.

- **Avoiding Exploitation:** Emphasize the importance of working with trusted, fiduciary advisors.

- **Diverse Experts:** Presenters should reflect the demographics of the retiree community they serve.

Call to Action:

Take charge of your financial future and create a legacy that reflects your values. Explore Personal Finance and Legacy Planning seminars today!

89

Creative Problem-Solving Workshops

Creative Problem-Solving Workshops: Unleash Innovative Solutions

Brief Description:

BREAK FREE FROM CONVENTIONAL thinking and discover surprisingly effective problem-solving methods. Our interactive workshops will teach you out-of-the-box techniques, playful brainstorming strategies, and how to apply them to both personal and real-world challenges.

Why It's Great for Retirees:

- **Mental Agility:** Keep your mind sharp and adaptable with a fun, engaging challenge.

- **Beyond Crosswords:** Expand your problem-solving toolkit beyond your usual go-to methods.

- **Real-World Relevance:** Learn techniques with applications from home improvement to community issues.

- **Rediscover Playfulness:** Tap into your inner innovator in a relaxed, supportive environment.

Getting Started:

- **Workshop Intensity:** Options range from short, idea-focused sessions to multi-part courses with more practice.

- **Open to Experimentation:** These are about the process, not always finding the 'right' answer immediately.

- **Diverse Examples:** Workshops should illustrate the techniques applied to problems big and small.

Resources Needed:

- **Notebook and Pens:** Capture ideas, sketch solutions, and jot down unexpected connections.

- **Creative Fuel:** Some workshops might playfully incorporate art supplies, building materials, etc.

- **Collaborative Spirit:** Be open to bouncing ideas off others and building on unconventional suggestions.

Challenges and Tips:

- **Letting Go of Perfection:** It's about the journey of creative thought, not always a polished end product.

- **Embracing Weirdness:** The best solutions might initially seem off-the-wall – that's part of the process!

- **Focus on Application:** Ensure the workshop also teaches how to adapt these techniques to your own life.

Ways to Deepen the Experience:

- **Guest Facilitators:** Invite entrepreneurs or artists to share how they approach obstacles creatively.

- **Community Challenge:** Tackle a local issue as a group, applying the workshop's methods.

- **Innovation Showcase:** Celebrate the wild solutions devised, even if purely hypothetical, to inspire further thinking.

Safety and Accessibility:

- **Respectful Debate:** Ensure diverse ideas are welcomed, and critiquing a solution isn't critiquing the person.

- **All Skill Levels:** Welcome both "I'm not creative!" types and those who want to hone their existing skills.

- **Physical Considerations:** Activity level should be clear upfront (if building prototypes, etc.).

Call to Action:

Ready to think outside the box? Explore Creative Problem-Solving Workshops and surprise yourself with the innovative solutions you generate!

90

Public Speaking and Storytelling Clubs

Public Speaking and Storytelling Clubs: Find Your Voice, Share Your Story

Brief Description:

CONQUER STAGE FRIGHT, BECOME a captivating storyteller, and connect with a supportive community in our dynamic speaking clubs. Through structured practice, coaching, and the chance to share your unique experiences, you'll gain the confidence to express yourself with power and authenticity.

Why It's Great for Retirees:

- **Self-Discovery:** Uncover hidden talents and gain insight into your own personal story.

- **Communication Boost:** Whether it's giving toasts, advocating for a cause, or sharing wisdom, refine your delivery.

- **Combat Isolation:** Build meaningful connections with fellow speakers and supportive audiences.

- **Legacy Building:** Hone the skills to pass down family stories, insights, or become a public voice on issues you care about.

Getting Started:

- **Club Format:** Choose groups that match your goals – formal practice, themed storytelling nights, or a mix.

- **Experience Levels:** Find clubs that welcome both novices and those with some speaking experience.

- **Positive Atmosphere:** Prioritize a culture of constructive feedback, encouragement, and celebration of progress.

Resources Needed:

- **Prepared Pieces (Optional):** Some clubs focus on impromptu speaking, others allow for short prepared speeches.

- **Notebook:** To draft ideas, record feedback, and note what resonates in other speakers' presentations.

- **Willingness to Grow:** A desire to improve, and the courage to step outside your comfort zone.

Challenges and Tips:

- **Vulnerability:** Sharing your story takes bravery, but the supportive environment makes it easier.

- **It's Not Stand-Up:** Focus on honest expression over forced humor, authenticity is key.

- **Pacing Yourself:** Start with short pieces, building confidence gradually over time.

Ways to Deepen the Experience:

- **Skills Workshops:** Supplement club meetings with sessions on body language, vocal techniques, etc.

- **Community Showcases:** Organize public events where members can share their honed stories.

- **Cross-Generational Collaboration:** Partner with youth groups for storytelling exchanges and mentorship.

Safety and Accessibility:

- **Respectful Feedback:** Clear guidelines to ensure critiques are constructive and never personal.

- **Diverse Stories:** Actively encourage participation from a wide range of backgrounds and experiences.

- **Accommodations:** Ensure venues are accessible and inquire about options for those with hearing or speech difficulties.

Call to Action:

Ready to unlock your communication potential? Join a Public Speaking and Storytelling Club and discover the transformative power of sharing your voice!

91

Cultural Competency and Language Immersion

Cultural Competency and Language Immersion: Your Passport to Global Connection

BRIEF DESCRIPTION: EXPAND YOUR horizons and deepen your understanding of the world through immersive programs that combine language learning with cultural exploration. Gain practical communication skills while developing a nuanced appreciation for diverse perspectives and ways of life.

Why It's Great for Retirees:

- **Purposeful Travel:** Turn a vacation into a transformative experience with a focus on genuine interaction.

- **Combat Misconceptions:** Challenge stereotypes and gain firsthand insights into other cultures.

- **Mental Stimulation:** Language learning keeps your mind sharp and builds new neural pathways.

- **Lifelong Friendships:** Connect with locals and fellow travelers who share your passion for cultural exchange.

Getting Started:

- **Language Choice:** Pick a language that sparks your curiosity or aligns with your travel dreams.

- **Immersion Level:** Options range from intensive language courses to programs with cultural excursions.

- **Location, Location:** Learn in bustling cities, quaint villages, or retreat settings for different vibes.

Resources Needed:

- **Beginner's Mindset:** Even a few basic phrases and willingness to learn go a long way.

- **Cultural Guidebook:** Supplement language learning with information about traditions and social norms.

- **Open Heart:** A genuine desire to connect with people from backgrounds different from your own.

Challenges and Tips:

- **The Learning Curve:** Language acquisition takes time, be patient with yourself and celebrate small wins.

- **Beyond the Classroom:** Seek out opportunities to practice in real-world settings (markets, cafes, etc.).

- **Respectful Engagement:** Learn about local customs and etiquette to avoid unintentional faux pas.

Ways to Deepen the Experience:

- **Homestay Option:** Live with a local family for the most immersive experience.

- **Community Projects:** Participate in volunteer projects that foster real interaction and exchange.Opens in a new windowwww.southernstar.ietraveler volunteering at a local garden or school.

- **Themed Programs:** Choose options focused on art, cuisine, or specific cultural celebrations.

Safety and Accessibility:

- **Reputable Schools:** Prioritize programs with experienced teachers and positive student reviews.

- **Age Inclusivity:** Seek out groups with diverse age ranges or those specifically designed for mature learners.

- **Health Considerations:** Choose locations with good healthcare access and address any mobility needs.

Call to Action:

Ready to become a global citizen? Explore Cultural Competency and Language Immersion programs and unlock a world of meaningful connections!

92

Strategic Board Game Leagues

Strategic Board Game Leagues: Outsmart, Outmaneuver, Outlast Your Opponents

Brief Description:

REDISCOVER THE THRILL OF classic strategy games and ignite your competitive spirit! Join our leagues for games like chess, Go, bridge, and other mentally stimulating classics. Challenge yourself, forge new friendships, and showcase your strategic mastery.

Why It's Great for Retirees:

- **Brain Power Workout:** Keep your mind sharp, improve focus, and enhance problem-solving skills.

- **Social Connection:** Bond with fellow enthusiasts over shared love of strategic thinking.

- **A Touch of Competition:** Enjoy the thrill of victory and the camaraderie of good sportsmanship.

- **Legacy Games:** Learn timeless games steeped in history and rich with tradition.

Getting Started:

- **Skill Levels:** Leagues often have divisions (beginner, intermediate, advanced) for fair matchups.

- **Game Choice:** Focus on your favorite or branch out and learn a new classic strategy game.

- **Format:** Tournaments, ongoing ladders, or casual meetups – pick a style that suits you.

Resources Needed:

- **The Game Set:** You might own it, or the league may provide boards and pieces.

- **Strategy Resources:** Books, online tutorials, or even seasoned players as mentors to up your game.

- **Good Sportsmanship:** Grace in victory and defeat are essential to the friendly league spirit.

Challenges and Tips:

- **Finding Opponents:** Leagues solve this! Perfect if you lack regular people to play against.

- **Welcoming Newbies:** Ensure there are entry points for those less familiar with a particular game.

- **Keeping it Fun:** Balance the competitive element with a focus on enjoyment and learning.

Ways to Deepen the Experience:

- **Game Analysis Sessions:** Dissect famous matches or have experts break down winning strategies.

- **Themed Tournaments:** Historical dress-up chess, blitz Go challenges, etc., can add playful elements.

- **Beyond the Board:** Organize game-themed outings (museum exhibits on chess, a film about a Go master, etc.).

Safety and Accessibility:

- **Respectful Environment:** Zero tolerance for disruptive behavior, ensuring everyone feels comfortable.

- **Noise Levels:** Choose venues conducive to focus, with options for quieter spaces if needed.

- **Adaptive Equipment:** Consider large-print cards, etc., for those with visual or dexterity needs.

Call to Action:

Ready to flex your strategic muscles? Seek out Strategic Board Game Leagues and let the games begin!

Sports and Games

93

Outdoor Adventure Races

Outdoor Adventure Races: Explore, Strategize, Conquer!

Brief Description:

GET YOUR ADRENALINE PUMPING and test your teamwork with our exhilarating adventure races! Combining navigation, outdoor skills, and a dash of problem-solving, these unique challenges will take you through stunning natural landscapes. Choose your distance and intensity level, and get ready for an experience unlike any other.

Why It's Great for Retirees:

- **Scalable Challenge:** With varying difficulty levels, find a race that matches your fitness and thrill-seeking appetite.

- **Camaraderie and Fun:** Form a team with friends or meet like-minded adventurers along the way.

- **Nature Connection:** Discover hidden trails, scenic vistas, and the beauty of your local environment.

- **Mental and Physical Boost:** Exercise your mind and body with a unique, goal-oriented adventure.

Getting Started:

- **Race Format:** Checkpoint-based orienteering, multi-stage treks, or a mix of other outdoor activities (paddling, etc.).

- **Team or Solo:** Some races are team-focused, others welcome individual competitors.

- **Level Up Gradually:** If new to this, shorter, beginner-friendly races are a great starting point.

Resources Needed:

- **Fitness Base:** Training plans are often provided, ensuring you're race-ready.

- **Gear List:** From compasses to any specialized equipment required for the specific race.

- **Strategic Mind:** It's not just about speed – route planning and quick thinking are key.

Challenges and Tips:

- **Navigation Skills:** Brush up on map reading or take a basic orienteering course if needed.

- **Team Dynamics:** If racing as a team, practice communication and problem-solving together.

- **Adaptability:** Weather and surprises are part of the adventure, be ready to adjust your plans.

Ways to Deepen the Experience:

- **Training Hikes:** Organize group practice runs to test gear and build racing confidence.

- **Themed Races:** Costumes, historical routes, or a charity focus can add a sense of fun.

- **Post-Race Celebration:** Emphasize the shared accomplishment with a social gathering or awards ceremony.

Safety and Accessibility:

- **Detailed Safety Plan:** Reputable races prioritize clear routes, checkpoints, and emergency protocols.

- **Experienced Guides:** Support staff and seasoned racers on hand to assist if needed.

- **Inclusive Options:** Offer routes with varying distances and technical difficulty.

Call to Action:

Ready for an unforgettable adventure? Explore Outdoor Adventure Races and step into a world of exploration, challenge, and the thrill of crossing the finish line!

94

Water Sports Exploration

Water Sports Exploration: Experience the Joy of Calm Water Adventures

Brief Description:

DISCOVER THE SERENITY AND exhilaration of water sports in a safe and welcoming environment. Learn the basics of stand-up paddleboarding, canoeing, and kayaking on tranquil lakes or protected waterways. Embrace the beauty of being on the water, enhance your balance and fitness, and connect with a community of nature-loving enthusiasts.

Why It's Great for Retirees:

- **Low-Impact Exercise:** Build strength and improve balance in a way that's gentle on joints.

- **Stress Relief:** The rhythm of paddling and scenic surroundings offer a powerful stress buster.

- **Social and Supportive:** Learn alongside fellow adventurers, creating camaraderie and shared achievements.

- **New Horizons:** Explore your surroundings from a fresh perspective and access hidden natural gems.

Getting Started:

- **Introductory Classes:** Focus on foundational skills, safety techniques, and proper equipment use.

- **Calm Conditions:** Begin in protected bays, lakes, or slow-moving rivers to ease into the experience.

- **No Experience Needed:** These programs welcome beginners and prioritize a gentle learning process.

Resources Needed:

- **Gear and Guidance:** Programs often provide paddleboards, canoes, kayaks, and life vests.

- **Comfortable Clothing:** Dress for the weather and water conditions (swimsuits, quick-dry layers).

- **Sun Protection:** Hat, sunglasses, and sunscreen are essential for enjoyable time on the water.

Challenges and Tips:

- **Building Confidence:** Initial unsteadiness is normal! Start with shorter outings and focus on technique.

- **Fitness Level:** Choose activities that align with your abilities and gradually increase duration.

- **Respecting the Water:** Always prioritize safety and understand weather and water conditions.

Ways to Deepen the Experience:

- **Mindful Paddling:** Incorporate gentle stretching or meditation while on the water for added relaxation.

- **Nature Watching:** Bring binoculars for birdwatching and wildlife spotting during your excursions.

- **Photography Focus:** Capture the beauty of your surroundings from a unique waterborne perspective.

Safety and Accessibility:

- **Certified Instructors:** Ensure instructors have water safety and teaching qualifications.

- **Properly Fitted Gear:** Life vests and paddles must be the right size to ensure comfort and safety.

- **Inclusivity:** Offer adaptive equipment or modified activities for those with mobility limitations.

Call to Action:

Ready to make a splash? Explore Water Sports Exploration Programs and discover the tranquility and adventure of paddling!

95

Archery and Marksmanship Clubs

Archery and Marksmanship Clubs: Find Your Focus, Test Your Skill

Brief Description:

DISCOVER THE TIMELESS DISCIPLINES of archery and marksmanship in a safe and welcoming environment. Receive expert instruction on technique, equipment, and safety protocols. Develop focus, control, and enjoy the satisfaction of hitting your target.

Why It's Great for Retirees:

- **Mental and Physical Challenge:** Sharpen your hand-eye coordination, focus, and body awareness.

- **Stress Relief:** The rhythmic nature of the practice and focus on the target is incredibly calming.

- **Accessible and Adaptable:** With proper instruction, these sports can be enjoyed by people of various fitness levels.

- **Community Connection:** Bond with fellow archers and marksmen over a shared pursuit of skill and precision.

Getting Started:

- **Discipline Choice:** Focus on traditional archery, target archery, or opt for marksmanship (pistols, rifles).

- **Indoor/Outdoor Options:** Clubs might have their own range or partner with established facilities.

- **Instruction Focus:** Seek out clubs that prioritize beginner safety and technique development.

Resources Needed:

- **Equipment:** Clubs may provide initial equipment to try out before investing in your own.

- **Range/Club Fees:** Factor in costs of accessing ranges or any club membership dues.

- **Eye and Ear Protection:** Essential safety gear for marksmanship participants.

Challenges and Tips:

- **Finding the Right Fit:** Explore different bow styles or firearm types to find what feels best for you.

- **It's a Process:** Skill development takes time – celebrate small improvements, not just bullseyes.

- **Respect the Rules:** Safety is paramount, and good clubs will emphasize responsible practices.

Ways to Deepen the Experience:

- **Friendly Competitions:** Organized shoots or tournaments add a fun layer of challenge.

- **Cross-Training:** Incorporate strength and flexibility exercises to enhance your performance.

- **Mindset Matters:** Explore the mental aspect of the sport with books or resources on focus techniques.

Safety and Accessibility:

- **Certified Instructors:** Look for archery coaches or range safety officers with credentials.

- **Safe Storage:** Clubs must have secure protocols for any firearms when not in use.

- **Adaptability:** Clubs should be welcoming and offer guidance on modifications if needed.

Call to Action:

Ready to hone your aim and achieve mental clarity? Explore Archery and Marksmanship Clubs and discover the power of precision!

96

Golf Clinics and Mini-Tournaments

Golf Clinics and Mini-Tournaments: Elevate Your Game, Ignite Your Competitive Spirit

Brief Description:

TAKE YOUR GOLF SKILLS to the next level with our specialized clinics and lively mini-tournaments. Our expert instructors will provide advanced technique tips to address your specific swing challenges. Then, put your newfound skills to the test in friendly competition and celebrate your successes on the green.

Why It's Great for Retirees:

- **Sharpen Your Skills:** Target those tricky aspects of your game and gain actionable improvement strategies.

- **Camaraderie and Challenge:** Enjoy the social side of golf, fostering connection and a fun competitive spirit.

- **Course Strategy:** Learn tips for reading greens, shot selection, and managing the mental game.

- **Celebrate Progress:** Mini-tournaments are a chance to see your improvement in action and recognize others' successes.

Getting Started:

- **Skill Focus Clinics:** Choose clinics that match your needs (putting, short game, specialty shots, etc.).

- **Tournament Format:** Opt for formats that are fun and pressure-free (scrambles, best ball, etc.).

- **Convivial Atmosphere:** Seek a club atmosphere that prioritizes both skill refinement and friendly rivalry.

Resources Needed:

- **Your Clubs and Gear:** Ensure you have all your equipment ready for clinics and the tournament.

- **Golf Etiquette:** Brush up on the finer points to ensure a smooth, enjoyable tournament experience.

- **Competitive Resolve:** Bring your best game, but keep a focus on fun and sportsmanship.

Challenges and Tips:

- **Realistic Expectations:** Clinics won't magically fix everything, but they offer targeted improvement pathways.

- **Matchup Fairness:** If skill levels vary widely, tournaments might use handicaps or tiered divisions.

- **Beyond the Scores:** Appreciate the social aspect win or lose; it's about the shared love of the game.

Ways to Deepen the Experience:

- **Guest Instructors:** Bring in a pro for a special clinic, offering fresh insights on technique or strategy.

- **Post-Tournament Social:** A 19th hole gathering keeps the fun going and deepens the community.

- **Skills Challenges:** Add side challenges during the tournament for prizes or bragging rights (closest to the pin, etc.).

Safety and Accessibility:

- **Warm-Up Emphasis:** Clinics should include injury prevention techniques specific to golfers.

- **Inclusive Atmosphere:** Ensure players of diverse skill levels feel welcome in the tournaments.

- **Cart Options:** Consider golf carts for those who want them, even in shorter tournaments.

Call to Action:

Ready to level up your golf game? Join our Golf Clinics and Mini-Tournaments and discover the satisfaction of continuous improvement!

97

Bicycle Touring Clubs

Bicycle Touring Clubs: Explore, Pedal, Connect

Brief Description:

REDISCOVER THE JOY OF travel by bicycle! Join our community of cycling enthusiasts as we embark on scenic tours ranging from delightful day trips to multi-day adventures. Explore hidden gems, connect with fellow riders, and challenge yourself on two wheels.

Why It's Great for Retirees:

- **Active Exploration:** Combine fitness, sightseeing, and the satisfaction of self-powered travel.

- **Varied Routes:** Cater to all fitness levels, from leisurely spins to more challenging climbs.

- **Shared Passion:** Bond with like-minded cyclists who appreciate adventure on two wheels.

- **Logistics Support:** Some clubs can assist with route planning, gear advice, and even transport for longer trips.

Getting Started:

- **Tour Length & Intensity:** Match your abilities and goals to ensure an enjoyable experience.

- **Bike Type:** Road bikes, hybrids, or touring bikes are all options depending on the terrain.

- **Solo or Guided:** Clubs may offer organized group rides or simply connect members for self-planned trips.

Resources Needed:

- **Roadworthy Bike:** Ensure a good fit and that it's properly maintained for the distances you'll tackle.

- **Essential Gear:** Helmet, repair kit, panniers (if carrying luggage), clothing for changing weather.

- **Ride Fuel:** Snacks, hydration, and knowledge of resupply points along the planned route.

Challenges and Tips:

- **Gradual Build-Up:** If new to touring, start with shorter rides to gain fitness and confidence.

- **Safety First:** Obey traffic laws, ride predictably, and use lights for visibility.

- **Buddy System:** Especially on longer rides, having a cycling partner is safer and more fun.

Ways to Deepen the Experience:

- **Themed Rides:** Culinary tours (farm stops, wineries), history routes, or following scenic rail trails.

- **Skills Workshops:** Tire repair clinics, navigation tech, or bikepacking optimization.

- **Multi-Modal Adventures:** Combine cycling with train travel to explore further afield.

Safety and Accessibility:

- **Route Safety:** Prioritize bike paths or roads with good shoulders, especially on group rides.

- **Support Vehicle:** Options for longer tours can be vital for rest breaks or if issues arise.

- **Inclusivity:** Offer routes of varying difficulty to accommodate diverse fitness levels.

Call to Action:

Ready to leave the ordinary behind? Join a Bicycle Touring Club and discover the world by pedal power!

98

Lawn Games and Socials

Lawn Games and Socials: Fun, Friendship, and a Little Friendly Rivalry

Brief Description:

Rediscover the timeless charm of classic lawn games! Join us for afternoons of bocce, croquet, lawn bowling, and other easy-to-learn favorites. Embrace the spirit of playful competition, enjoy refreshments, and connect with neighbors in a relaxed, outdoor setting.

Why It's Great for Retirees:

- **Gentle Exercise:** Get moving and enjoy some fresh air without overly strenuous activity.

- **Social Connection:** Play, mingle, and make new friends in your community.

- **Low-Pressure Fun:** Games are easy to pick up, no prior experience required, just a willingness to laugh!

- **Nostalgia Factor:** Rekindle memories of backyard games from childhood or summers past.

Getting Started:

- **Venue:** Parks, community centers, or even spacious backyards are perfect settings.

- **Game Rotation:** Offer a mix of games to cater to different interests and skill levels.

- **Welcoming to All:** Emphasize that these events are about camaraderie, not cutthroat rivalry.

Resources Needed:

- **The Games:** Clubs or organizers should provide sets of bocce, croquet mallets, etc.

- **Refreshments:** Keep it simple with lemonade, snacks, and a space for people to gather and chat.

- **Shade** Consider tents or choosing locations with trees for comfort on sunny days.

Challenges and Tips:

- **Accessibility:** Choose a venue with easy access and relatively flat playing surfaces.

- **Teaching the Basics:** Have a designated person quickly explain the rules of each game to newcomers.

- **Weather Watch:** Have a backup indoor space, or be flexible in rescheduling if weather is a factor.

Ways to Deepen the Experience:

- **Vintage Vibes:** Encourage whimsical attire (hats, whites for croquet) for extra amusement.

- **Potluck Element:** Invite attendees to contribute a favorite snack or drink to share.

- **Beyond the Games:** Simple yard games like cornhole or giant Jenga add to the options.

Safety and Accessibility:

- **Hydration Stations:** Ensure people have ample access to water, especially on warm days.

- **Seating:** Provide benches or chairs for those who wish to rest between games.

- **Inclusive Atmosphere:** Encourage a playful attitude and ensure no one feels excluded.

Call to Action:

Ready for some lighthearted outdoor fun? Join our Lawn Games and Socials and embrace the joy of simple pleasures!

99

Fantasy Sports and Analytics

Fantasy Sports and Analytics: Outsmart Your League, Decode the Stats

Brief Description:

DIVE DEEPER INTO THE world of fantasy sports, where statistical analysis is your secret weapon! Whether you're a seasoned player or a curious newcomer, develop data-driven strategies for drafting teams, setting lineups, and making those crucial trades.

Why It's Great for Retirees:

- **Mental Workout:** Sharpen your math skills, statistical understanding, and strategic decision-making.

- **Passion Meets Purpose:** Turn your love for sports into an engaging mind-bending challenge.

- **The Community of Experts:** Bond with a like-minded group, dissecting data, and debating strategy.

- **Bragging Rights:** Elevate your fantasy game and outwit even the most seasoned competitors.

Getting Started:

- **Sport of Choice:** Focus on popular fantasy leagues: football, baseball, basketball, etc.

- **Beginner to Advanced:** Tailor programs based on existing analytics knowledge and desired depth.

- **Tools of the Trade:** Introduce free and paid sports analytics platforms, spreadsheets, etc.

Resources Needed:

- **Reliable Data:** Source reputable sports statistics websites and analysis tools.

- **League/Platform:** Choose an existing fantasy league or create a custom one for the group.

- **Instructional Focus:** Do you provide the analytics or is it collaborative learning and discovery?

Challenges and Tips:

- **Time Investment:** Fantasy sports and in-depth analysis can be a significant commitment.

- **Data Overload:** Start with key metrics, then gradually expand your statistical understanding.

- **The Luck Factor:** Even with the best analyses, sports retain an element of unpredictability!

Ways to Deepen the Experience:

- **Guest "Experts":** Invite sports statisticians or experienced fantasy analysts for advanced sessions.

- **Mock Drafts:** Practice decision-making under pressure and debate draft strategy with the group.

- **"Moneyball" Angle:** Explore how statistics are used by real sports teams for player evaluation.

Safety and Accessibility:

- **Safe Learning Space:** Emphasize that it's friendly competition and mistakes are part of learning.

- **Technical Support:** Help less tech-savvy members learn to navigate fantasy platforms and tools.

- **Controlling the Stakes:** Keep any buy-ins low, prioritizing the love of the 'game' over financial risk.

Call to Action:

Ready to unleash your inner sports statistician? Explore Fantasy Sports and Analytics programs and take your game to a whole new level!

100

Martial Arts for Mind and Body

Martial Arts for Mind and Body: Discover Strength, Focus, and Inner Balance

Brief Description:

EMBARK ON A JOURNEY of self-improvement through martial arts designed for all fitness levels. Enhance flexibility, coordination, and mental focus while building core strength. Our classes offer a safe, supportive environment where you can cultivate a powerful connection between your mind and body.

Why It's Great for Retirees:

- **Improved Physical Health:** Gain confidence in your movement, build strength, and enhance balance.

- **Sharpened Mental Focus:** Practice discipline, cultivate mindfulness, and find a sense of inner calm.

- **Stress Relief:** Release pent-up tension through controlled movement and focused breathing.

- **Community and Support:** Train alongside others on a similar journey of self-discovery.

Getting Started:

- **Martial Arts Styles:** Options like Tai Chi, modified judo, or forms-based karate prioritize gentle, flowing movements.

- **Beginner-Centered:** Seek classes explicitly focused on adults new to martial arts, with an emphasis on proper form and injury prevention.

- **Experienced Instructors:** Look for teachers with patience, and a focus on the mind-body benefits.

Resources Needed:

- **Comfortable Clothing:** Loose-fitting attire that allows for a full range of motion.

- **Open Mind:** Embrace the challenge of learning new movement patterns and focus techniques.

- **Water Bottle:** Stay hydrated during practice.

Challenges and Tips:

- **It's a Journey:** Focus on consistent progress over quick mastery, and embrace the process of learning.

- **Listen to Your Body:** Honor your limits and communicate any physical concerns to the instructor.

- **Leave Ego at the Door:** This is about personal growth, not competition or comparison to others.

Ways to Deepen the Experience:

- **Meditation Integration:** Begin or end class with guided meditation to enhance mindfulness.

- **Philosophy and History:** Discuss the origins and philosophy behind your chosen martial art.

- **Mindful Modifications:** Instructors should demonstrate how to adapt movements for varying abilities.

Safety and Accessibility:

- **Safe Training Space:** Classes should be held in a spacious area with protective flooring if necessary.

- **Individualized Attention:** Teachers ensure everyone is using proper techniques to avoid injury.

- **Age-Inclusive Environment:** Emphasize that all ages and fitness levels are welcome.

Success Story:

Sarah struggled with balance issues. Tai Chi gave her confidence in her movements and relieved chronic stress.

Call to Action:

Ready to awaken your inner strength and cultivate physical and mental resilience?
Explore Martial Arts for Mind and Body classes today!
Let me know if you'd like a focus on a specific martial arts discipline!

Adventure Golfing

Adventure Golfing: Escape the Ordinary, Embrace the Unexpected

Brief Description:

REDISCOVER THE JOY OF golf with a twist! Venture beyond traditional courses to experience the thrill of night golf with glowing balls, the challenge of quirky landscapes, and the pure fun of the unexpected. Embrace a spirit of adventure and let your inner child loose on the links.

Why It's Great for Retirees:

- **Break the Routine:** Add a spark of excitement to your golfing routine and challenge yourself in new ways.

- **Novel Experiences:** Create lasting memories by golfing under the stars or tackling whimsical, themed courses.

- **Social Fun:** Perfect for groups of friends seeking a shared adventure with a generous dose of laughter.

- **All Skill Levels:** Many adventure golfing experiences prioritize enjoyment over perfect scores.

Getting Started:

- **Seek Out the Unusual:** Look for courses featuring glow-in-the-dark golf, miniature golf with elaborate themes, or scenic courses set in unique locales (beaches, mountains, etc.).

- **Match the Intensity:** Select courses catering to your desired level of physical challenge and exertion.

- **Embrace Playfulness:** Leave perfectionism behind, focus on having a good time, and expect surprises.

Resources Needed:

- **Open Mind:** Be ready to giggle at the absurdity and embrace the unconventional shots you'll take.

- **Sense of Humor:** Unexpected bounces and lost balls are part of the adventure – laugh it off!

- **Gear Varies:** Check if the adventure venue provides specific equipment or if you bring your own.

Challenges and Tips:

- **Availability Varies:** This niche may require travel, or seeking out seasonal events near you.

- **Embrace the Dark:** Night golf requires adjustment – go slow at first and focus on enjoying the novelty.

- **Let Loose:** Perfect form isn't the goal here; enjoy trying weird shots and creative solutions.

Ways to Deepen the Experience:

- **Costume Element** Encourage themed attire (neon for night golf, pirate garb for a seaside mini-golf, etc.).

- **Photo Ops:** Unique courses and glow-in-the-dark equipment make for memorable photos.

- **Beyond the 'Golf':** Combine your outing with a quirky local dining experience for a full day of fun.

Safety and Accessibility:

- **Night Visibility:** Courses offering glow golf should have clear path markings for safety.

- **Ask About Terrain:** Ensure any 'extreme' courses are navigable if mobility is an issue.

- **Sun Protection:** For desert, beach, or unusual landscape golf, prioritize sun safety accordingly.

Call to Action:

Epilogue

It's not just about leisurely mornings and endless rounds of golf (unless that's truly your dream!). Retirement is your chance to rewrite the rules. To tackle that bucket list you never had time for. To say "yes" to adventures that make your heart beat a little faster. To learn, to create, to connect with people and passions that fill your days with purpose and a whole lot of fun.

You've put in the years, earned your freedom, and frankly, you deserve to make the most of every single day. This book has been your inspiration toolbox, giving you 101 ways to break free of the expected and design a retirement that's uniquely, wonderfully YOU.

So, are you ready? To laugh louder than you have in years? To dust off those dancing shoes or finally learn to speak that language? To make new friends and create memories to treasure? Retirement isn't merely a finish line, it's the most exciting starting block of your life. Now go out there and run your own extraordinary race!